Belize

BOOK

OF

LISTS

2000

LAN SLUDER

Belize Book of Lists 2000

Published by Equator Publications/Asheville.
Printed in the United States of America

Cover design by Keith Leonard.

Front and back cover photos (except scuba diver) copyright 1999 Tony Rath Photography, www.trphoto.com, www.belizenet.com, used by permission. Other photos also are used by permission and are the property of the original copyright owners.

ISBN: 0-9670488-0-X

For subscribers to BELIZE FIRST MAGAZINE, *Belize Book of Lists 2000* is Vol. IV, No. 4 of BELIZE FIRST, the # 1 magazine on travel, life and retirement on the Caribbean Coast.

ISSN 1521-2815
Web edition of Belize First Magazine at www.turq.com/belizefirst/.

270 Beaverdam Road • Candler, NC 28715 USA • Fax 828-667-1717
e-mail: BZEFIRST@aol.com • Web: www.turq.com/belizefirst/

A New Kind of Guide to Belize

By LAN SLUDER
Editor and Publisher
BELIZE FIRST MAGAZINE

Think of the *Belize Book of Lists 2000* as a new kind of guidebook. This guide boils down gallons of information about Belize into easy-to-swallow gulps, short lists of the top 5 or 10 in each category, such as best dive sites or best beaches, with a bit of supporting detail on each item. This is also a guidebook that's not afraid to make judgments about the best of the Caribbean Coast. We go out on a limb to list the best hotels, best restaurants, best sightseeing, best places. And, by inference, what's not so good.

Am I always right? Of course not. Will you always agree with my selections? I doubt it. It's not always easy ranking and distinguishing among several excellent choices. Hard cases, Judge Learned Hand said, make bad law. Better, however, I say, to give you a candid opinion, than to waffle like a weasel.

The opinions in the *Belize Book of Lists 2000* are based on my personal experiences in Belize. I've visited nearly all of the hotels, restaurants and places listed here. The information also is based on the opinion of travel writers I trust, and on the reports and comments of many BELIZE FIRST readers.

The main purpose of the *Belize Book of Lists 2000* is to answer your questions about Belize, whether you're planning a first trip to this fascinating country, visiting for the 10th time, or considering relocating permanently.

If, for example, you are wondering about the best jungle lodges in Belize, just turn to page 85 and read about the 10 Top Jungle Lodges. If you're interesting in learning what there is to see and do in Belize, check out 5 Reasons to Visit Belize (page 8), 5 Reasons NOT to Visit Belize (page 9), 5 "Must-See" Maya Sites (page 94) or 10 Best Museums, Nature and Historical Attractions (page 95). If you're going to Ambergris Caye, Belize's most popular destination, see the lists on pages 79 to 83. If you're trying to make sense out of the bewildering variety of choices in a trip to Belize, look at the section on planning your Belize trip (pages 23 to 44.)

Rather than try to put addresses and other contact information with each listing, we've consolidated all those in one section, Contacts, which follows the lists. Wherever you ramble in Belize, I hope this guide helps you have a better experience.

Table of Contents

Photo by Sheila M. Lambert

Why Belize?

Photo by Lan Sluder

British, Belize and American flags fly over the entrance to the Radisson Fort George, Belize City

5 Reasons to Visit Belize

Belize isn't for everyone. But what it does offer, it offers in glorious plenty.

1 Diving/snorkeling
Regardless of your level of ability or physical condition, there's a place and mask for you in Belize. The Diving around the atolls is world-class, excellent on the reef off Stann Creek and Toledo districts, and not bad even around the more-visited parts of the barrier reef near Ambergris Caye. Snorkeling is also excellent, though except from the cayes directly on or near the reef such as South Water, Tobacco, Goff's and English, it requires a short boat ride to the reef. A caution, though: The Caribbean here can see rough seas, making snorkeling iffy on windy or stormy days. Long dive boat rides can be a queasy experience, Mate.

2 Maya sites
Belize was the heart of the Maya world, and today dozens of ruins can be visited without the hordes of tourists common in Mexico and elsewhere in the region. Among the most interesting ruins in Belize for the non-archeologist visitor are Lamanai, Caracol, Xunantunich, Cahal Pech, El Pilar and Lubaantun.

3 Ecotravel: Birds, wildlife, and nature
Most of Belize remains lightly populated by humans and untouched by developers, so it is a paradise for wild critters and birds. More than 500 species of birds have been spotted in Belize. The country has as many as 700 species of butterflies. Animals rare or extinct elsewhere still thrive in Belize's bush. Nature is still natural here. A surprising number of Belizeans have a real commitment to protecting the environment.

4 Adventure
Belize is a great place for adventure, soft or otherwise. Come for hiking, canoeing, kayaking, wind surfing and caving. Indeed, Belize offers some of the best spelunking anywhere, with huge cave systems, some yet unexplored, in the Maya Mountains and elsewhere.

5 Culture
No, not the kind you get from museums; Belize offers visitors a laboratory of human culture, all in a small and accessible space. Belize is a truly multi-racial, multi-cultural, multi-lingual society. Far from perfect, with dangers as well as pleasures, a trip to Belize can be an education. Come with your eyes, and mind, open.

5 Reasons NOT to Visit Belize

If you love Cancun, you probably won't like Belize.

1 Golf and Tennis
Although the British played golf here in British Honduras days, the only golf in Belize now is a new 9-hole course on Caye Chapel and a small private course near Orange Walk Town. A couple of other courses are in the blue-sky planning stage. Only two hotels in Belize have tennis courts.

2 Shopping
Shopping in Belize may remind you of Hobbes' description of working class life in Olde England — nasty, brutal and short. While there are several modern supermarkets and stores in Belize City, and a few shops of visitor interest in San Pedro and Cayo and elsewhere, prices for almost everything but rum are high and selection is limited. Neither does Belize have the rich craft tradition of its neighbors Guatemala and Mexico.

3 Great beaches
Those coming to Belize expecting the wide white sandy beaches of Anguilla, the British Virgin Islands or parts of Mexico's Yucatán are likely to be disappointed. The barrier reef all along the coast of Belize provides for rich underwater life but also blocks the sand deposits of less-protected shores. Seagrass is common off most beaches. Ambergris Caye has some small, human-helped beaches, the small ribbons of sand at Hopkins/Sittee Point and Placencia/Seine Bight/Maya Beach are pleasant, and several of the remote cayes have postcard-style strips of sandy beach, but no beach in Belize would make the world's top 100 list.

4 Nightlife
If you like to party hard, consider going elsewhere. Outside of hotels and a couple of restaurant lounges, Belize City offers little besides gritty local bars and clubs. San Pedro has the most action, what with the chicken drop at the Spindrift Hotel, and about 20 bars, some of which blast 'til the wee hours. At the jungle lodges and remote resorts, guests are usually in bed by nine or ten, tired from the day's activities. Weekends see some bar action in towns such as PG, Corozal and San Ignacio. Houses of ill repute have suffered since the downsizing of the British Army in Belize, but there are brothels in Belize City, Cayo, Orange Walk and elsewhere. *Caveat emptor.*

5 Gourmet dining
Contrary to rumors, you CAN get a satisfying meal in Belize, even an excellent one, but *Guide Michelin* will not need to come to Belize anytime soon.

10 Frequently Asked Questions on Belize

Here are the questions we get most often from first-time travelers to Belize (other than questions on specific hotels), along with abbreviated versions of our answers.

1 "Is it safe?"

Yes, with routine precautions, Belize is as safe as most vacation destinations. Drugs, unemployment, the large percentage of Belizeans in the high-crime teenage and young-adult years, and the influence of U.S. television and culture contribute to crime in Belize City, Orange Walk Town, Dangriga and elsewhere, but Belize police do their best to stop criminals and solve crimes, which is more than you can say for many other countries in the region. The vast majority of visitors to Belize say they feel completely safe.

2 "What's the cheapest way to get to Belize?"

In most cases, the cheapest way to get to Belize from North America or Europe is is to fly into Cancun (the resort enclave which gets about 25 times as many visitors as all of Belize and thus has a lot of charter and low-fare air service) and then take a bus (comfortable, cheap and with amenities such as reserved seats and videos) for the six-hour ride to Chetumal at Belize's northern border. You can also fly into Cozumel and take a bus from Playa del Carmen.

3 "We want to relax at the beach but also see some of mainland Belize — where should we go?"

The classic "surf and turf" in Belize is a few days on Ambergris Caye (or Caye Caulker for budget travelers) and then a few days in Cayo. That's still a good option, especially for those with limited time, but there's plenty to see in most areas of Belize. Placencia is becoming an increasingly popular destination, though it's still sleepy off-season. For travelers who like to get a bit off the beaten track, Corozal and Orange Walk districts in the north are well worth exploring. Dangriga offers an interesting cultural experience, and the Hopkins/Sittee area to the south of Dangriga is friendly and not touristy. Toledo is Belize's frontier and a jumping off point for Caribbean Guatemala and Honduras. The quintessential Belize experience, however, may be a week on a remote caye, with nothing to do but doze in a hammock on the beach between dive or snorkel trips.

4 "Should we rent a car?"

Yes, if you can afford to do so. Having your own wheels gives you the chance to see areas of Belize you can't easily reach by bus. The tradeoff is that you miss some of the local flavor found on public transportation, and you may not get the benefit of local knowledge offered by Belize's many excellent licensed guides.

 # 5 "Where's a good place to snorkel directly from the beach?"
Belize has world-class snorkeling, but in most cases it requires a boat ride to the barrier reef. Among the exceptions are cayes such as South Water Caye and Tobacco Caye which are directly on or very near the reef. Other islands with snorkeling include Little Water, French Louis, Ranguana, Northeast and around the atolls at Turneffe, Glovers and Lighthouse.

 # 6 "Where's the best diving in Belize?"
The best diving is around the atolls far off the coast of Belize — Lighthouse, Glovers and Turneffe. The second-best diving is along the barrier reef from around Dangriga south. Recreational divers will enjoy the diving off Ambergris and Caulker.

 # 7 "We want to see a Maya ruin — which one should we see?"
If you have the time, see Caracol or Lamanai. If you don't have much time, see Xunantunich, Cahal Pech and Che Chem Ha cave in the west, or Altun Ha in the north. If you have at least a full day and preferably longer, do Tikal in Guatemala. But Belize has hundreds of ruins, often literally in someone's back yard. Belize, after all, was the heart of the ancient Maya world.

 # 8 "Is summer a bad time to visit — how hot and rainy is it?"
It depends on where and when you're going. In general, the farther south you go, the more rain you'll get, and the more months the wet season lasts. It's hotter inland than on the coast, where there's usually a trade wind or breeze blowing (though the winds occasionally die down, especially in late summer.) Indeed, the "dry season" in late spring is usually the hottest time of year in inland areas such as Cayo, and it is a time of forest fire risk. The "green season" in Belize isn't like the monsoon season in Asia. It's more like southern Florida where you may get rain or intense storms for a few hours, often in the night or in the early morning, and then periods of beautiful sunshine. The main effect is on dirt roads especially in the south, which at times become impassable. We actually prefer the off-season in Belize. There are fewer tourists, and prices are lower. There's no chance of chilling "Northers" as in the winter. If we had to pick a single time to come to Belize, it probably would be right after Easter through June, when prices drop, water viz is excellent, the tradewinds still are blowing, and it's still too early for hurricanes or severe tropical storms, although, as noted, it's usually hot and dry inland until the rains come, typically in June. Belize averages about one hurricane every ten years, usually hitting in late summer. Only about one in 20 hurricanes in the Atlantic and Caribbean actually make it to landfall in the Western Caribbean, so your odds are good.

 # 9 "Is Belize a good place for kids?"
Yes, if your kids can make their own entertainment and enjoy the water and the

outdoors. Belize has no malls or McDonald's restaurants.

10 "Do we need shots to come to Belize?"

None is required, unless coming from a Yellow Fever area, and in fact most heading to the cayes or to a posh jungle lodge don't get any. However, malaria is present in Belize, and if you're spending any time outside the main tourist areas, it's better to be safe than sorry, with chloroquine. Of course, the best prevention is to avoid getting bitten by the *Anopheles* mosquito — splash on the DEET and cover up, especially around dusk. Any traveler should be up-to-date on tetanus, diphtheria and measles, and sticks for Hep A and B can be a good idea for some. Dengue fever is occasionally present in Belize, but there's no preventive for it except avoiding the *Aedes aegypti* mosquito. For the late word, contact the Centers for Disease Control or your doctor.

5 Misconceptions about Travel in Belize

1 "Belize is Belize is Belize."

Fact: Belize is not one destination, but many. It enjoys tremendous diversity, in climate, topography, culture, people, scenery and in many other ways. By traveling only an hour or two, you can experience a great variety of scenery and ecosystems, from sandy cayes to South Pacific-style atolls, from lowland tropical rain forest to pine forests that remind many of the Southern Appalachians. You can enjoy luxurious condo suites or rough it in jungle camps. You can climb a Maya temple one day and dive the Blue Hole the next. Going to Ambergris Caye and going, say, to Dangriga is like going to two different countries.

2 "It's smart to avoid the rainy reason."

Fact: Generally, June through October is the wettest period in Belize. But rainfall amounts vary tremendously, from around 50 inches a year (a rate similar to most of the Southeastern U.S.) in northern Belize to more than 200 inches in parts of the south. The length of the season when rains are more common also varies depending on location. In the south, typically only February through May are "dry."   In much of central, western and northern Belize, and on the cayes, although precipitation amounts are usually greatest from June to October, the rainy season is not a well-defined single period, any more than you would speak of a "rainy season" in Atlanta, Georgia. Even during seasonal rains, it may rain only for an hour or two, with the rest of the day beautifully sunny. Again, except in the far south, it is rare for there to be a lot of rain day after day over a period of many days.   It can happen, just as it can happen in Kansas City or Ottawa, but it's not a regular feature of Belize's moderate sub-tropical climate. Besides, the "rainy season" in Belize is also the "green season," when the hills are lush and green, showers moderate the hot weather, and the risk of forest fires is low.

3 "I've heard Belize City isn't safe, and I don't even want to spend the night there."

Fact: Belize City does have a serious crime problem (though it rarely affects visitors) and sometimes street punks can be a pain, but the vast majority of people in Belize City are friendly, hard-working folks. Most people in Belize City live ordinary lives. They go to work or school, visit friends, go out for dinner or to hear some music. For them, this is their home, not a crime scene. In Belize City's suburbs are some of the best residential areas in the country. Belize City is the country's cultural, business, legal and transportation center. If you're traveling around Belize, or spending a lot of time in the country, you really can't avoid Belize City. Use the same kind of common-sense precautions that you would in any urban area, and you won't have a problem. You might even get to enjoy Belize City. It has many colorful and interesting buildings, some excellent restaurants, modern stores and a lot of people well worth getting to know.

4 "Belize is in the Caribbean, so it must have great beaches."

Fact: Much of Belize's mainland cost is marshy mangrove swamp, with no beaches at all. In many mainland and island areas where there are beaches, the barrier reef just off the shore cuts down on the wave action that, over geological time, creates the wide, sandy beaches you see in some other areas of the Caribbean. That's not to say that you can't enjoy the beach life in Belize — swinging in a hammock by the sea, with sand between your toes, watching the coco palms sway in the breeze. There are attractive beach and waterfront areas on many of Belize's cayes, and on the mainland in Corozal and Stann Creek districts. But great beaches? They're rare in Belize.

5 "Belize is expensive."

Fact: There's a wide spectrum of costs for travel in Belize. At the low end, you can find clean, safe rooms in almost every area of Belize for under US$20 a day. You can also pay US$200 a day and up for deluxe international-style accommodations. Belize is particularly well equipped with quality accommodations in the moderate price range, family-run hotels in interesting locales where a couple can spend the night in comfort for under US$100. While auto rentals are more expensive in Belize than in many other destinations, buses are easy to use and cheap — you can travel from one end of Belize to the other for US$15. Internal air service is convenient and moderately priced. Most Belize restaurants are in the medium range, and you can always find a hearty meal of stew chicken and rice and beans for a few bucks. It's also important to note that while you can find cheaper places to vacation, Belize has high standards of health and hygiene, English is widely spoken, and most hotels and tourism operators offer value for your money.

About Belize

Kids on Caye Caulker take a break from selling bread to mug for the camera

10 Vital Dates in Belize History

300–
900 AD   Classic Maya period, when what is now Belize was the heart of the Maya empire with a population of one million.

1508   First Europeans — Spaniards — come to Belize; Maya resist.

1798   Baymen defeat Spanish at Battle of St. George's Caye on September 10, Belize's national day.

1838   Slaves emancipated.

1862   Britain declares British Honduras a colony and a member of British Commonwealth.

1931   Worst hurricane in Belize history strikes on September 10, kills about 2,000.

1949   Protests against devaluation of British Honduras dollar lead to formation of People's United Party headed by George Price, sowing seeds of independence.

1961   Hurricane Hattie nearly levels Belize City on the night before Halloween, kills more than 250.

1973   Name changed to Belize; capital moved to Belmopan from Belize City.

1981   On September 21, Belize becomes fully independent member of British Commonwealth.

10 Who Made Modern Belize

Here, in a very subjective listings, are 10 individuals and organizations which helped form and mold modern Belize.

1 George Cadle Price
A middle-class Catholic Creole, spartan, reclusive, considered incorruptible, George Price was a leader in the populist move for independence in the 1940s and 1950s; he founded the People's United Party and dominated it as party leader and prime minister for most of nearly half a century. Many consider him the George Washington of modern Belize.

2 Philip Goldson
With Price, Goldson was an early leader of the independence movement. He later headed an opposition group, National Independence Party, which eventually became the United Democratic Party.

3 Manuel Esquivel
Long-time head of the UDP, Esquivel was prime minister for two terms in the 1980s and 1990s.

4 Said Musa and Assad Shoman
The two are leaders of the "second generation" of Belize PUP politicos. Musa,

15

a British-educated lawyer, helped formed SPEAR (Society for the Promotion of Education and Research), an important political "think tank." He became prime minister in 1998. Shoman is a left-wing intellectual and author of *Thirteen Chapters of a History of Belize* and other books.

5 Evan X. Hyde and *Amandala*
As owner and editor of *Amandala* newspaper, Hyde helped focus Belize's attention on the black consciousness movement.

6 Owners of British Estate and Produce Company
In the 19th century, this company owned one-half the land in Belize, and its various directors and owners, mostly British or Scottish, remained powerful forces in Belize until the 1980s; Barry Bowen, a wealthy Belizean, bought the company and its then 709,000 acres in 1983.

7 James and Lydia Waight and the Belize Audubon Society
These and other founding members of the Belize Audubon Society, which began in 1969 as a part of the Florida Audubon Society and later became an independent organization, played a vital role in developing Belize's environmental consciousness.

8 Pioneers of Tourism
Vern Hammon's Reef Colony Resort, which opened in 1951, was the first resort on Ambergris Caye. Hammon and other early tourism pioneers such as Jerry McDermott, Ramon Nuñez, Celi McCorkle and Mick Fleming created an industry destined to be the # 1 business and hard currency earner in Belize.

9 Emory King
An American who was shipwrecked in Belize in 1953 and decided to stay, King became a successful businessman and one of Belize's most prolific authors. An early advocate for Belizean-owned businesses and tourism, he also was instrumental in bringing the Mennonites to Belize. Among his books are *Belize 1798 - The Road to Glory.* His latest job is Belize film commissioner.

10 Andy Palacio, Bredda David and Lord Rhaburn
These and other giants of punta, neo-brukdown, pan-Caribbean and cungo created the modern musical heritage of Belize.

5 Largest Cities and Towns in Belize

Population is roughly estimated as of the year 2000. Other population centers in Belize include Belmopan (7,000), Punta Gorda (5,000) and Ambergris Caye (5,000).

1 Belize City: 65,000

2 Orange Walk Town: 18,000
3 Corozal Town: 14,000
4 Dangriga: 13,000
5 San Ignacio/Santa Elena: 12,000

5 Key Facts about the Belize Economy

1 GDP

Belize's Gross Domestic Product in 1997 was US$567 million, or US$2,525 per capita. By comparison, per capita GDP in the U.S. was US$25,042. In 1997, Belize was ranked # 103 out of 191 countries in terms of GDP per capita. The entire Belize economy is about the size of the economy of a small U.S. town of fewer than 25,000 people.

2 Major Industries

Agriculture is the # 1 industry in Belize, contributing 20% of GDP and employing about 25% of the labor force. The main crops are sugar cane, bananas, citrus and corn. Tourism is the # 2 industry, representing about 17% of GDP. Tourism is expected to become the # 1 industry within the next few years. Overall, the services sector in Belize is the largest employer, employing about 61% of the labor force.

3 Imports/Exports

Belize imports more than it exports. In 1996, it exported US$166 million in goods, imported US$262 million, for a trade deficit of US$96 million. Belize's largest trade partner is the U.S.

4 Key Indicators

Annual inflation rate in Belize has averaged 3.2% in recent years, with the rate estimated as under 2% per year since 1997. Unemployment is estimated at 13% or more of the total work force of about 75,000. Local lending rates for loans are 16 to 18%. Belize has one telephone for every eight persons, and one television for every seven persons.

5 Government Sector

In 1997, the Belize government had revenues of US$162 million and expenditures of US$179 million, a deficit of about 9% of total spending. In 1996, Belize had an external debt of US$288 million, with annual debt service of US$40 million.

5 Largest Ethnic Groups in Belize

1 Mestizo: 44%

Persons of mixed European and Maya heritage, typically speaking Spanish as a first language and having social values more closely associated with Latin

America than with the Caribbean. Mestizos are concentrated in northern and western Belize. There is often a distinction made between Mestizos who came to Belize from the Yucatán during the Caste Wars of the mid-19th century and more-recent immigrants from Central America. Mestizos are the fastest-growing segment of the population.

#2 Creole: 30%
Persons usually but not always of African heritage, typically speaking Creole and English and often having a set of social values derived from England and the Caribbean. Creoles are concentrated in Belize City and Belize District, although there are predominantly Creole villages elsewhere, including the villages of Gales Point and Placencia.

#3 Maya: 11%
There are concentrations of Yucatec Maya in Corozal and Orange Walk districts, Mopan Maya in Toledo and Cayo districts, and Kekchí Maya in about 30 villages in Toledo.

#4 Garifuna: 7%
Garifuna (also known as Garinagu or Black Caribs) are of mixed African and Carib Indian heritage, most of whom came to then British Honduras from Honduras in 1832. Dangriga and Punta Gorda are towns with large Garifuna populations, as are the villages of Seine Bight, Hopkins and Barranco.

#5 Other: 8%
The "other" group in Belize includes several thousand Mennonites who came to Belize from Canada and Mexico in the 1950s. Divided into conservative and progressive groups, they farm large acreages in Belize. Conservatives live mostly in Shipyard, Barton Creek and Little Belize, avoid the use of modern farm equipment and speak German among themselves. Progressives live mostly in Blue Creek, Progresso and Spanish Lookout. Belize also has sizable communities of East Indians, who live mainly around Belize City and in Toledo, Chinese, mostly from Taiwan, living in Belize City, and "Anglos," mostly expats from the U.S. and Canada concentrated in San Pedro, Placencia, Cayo and around Corozal Town.

5 Best Sources of News about Belize
Journalism in Belize is free and free-wheeling, though the standards of news reporting are variable at best, and several of the newspapers are highly political. All of these can be easily accessed via www.belizenews.com.

1 Belize Channel 5/Great Belize Productions
Clearly the leader in Belize for unbiased, up-to-date news. It has a Web site

with transcripts of its weekday news broadcasts at www.channel5belize.com.

2 *The Reporter*
The best weekly newspaper (Belize has no daily papers) in the country. Web edition available.

3 *San Pedro Sun*
Friendly, chatty paper oriented to happenings on Ambergris Caye. Web edition available.

4 *Amandala*
Once Belize's feistiest journal, with a strong populist/black consciousness slant, Amandala isn't the paper it was, but it's regaining lost ground. Web edition available.

5 LOVE-FM Radio
Belize's leading radio station gets the news out, and there's a news summary available as an Internet mailing list.

10 Movers and Shakers in Today's Belize
(Listed alphabetically)
Michael Ashcroft
CEO, chairman and majority stockholder of the largest company based in Belize, Carlisle Holdings (formerly BHI Corp.) which owns Belize Bank, part of Belize Telecommunications, facilities management companies in the U.S., and other businesses. Ashcroft has the title of Belize Ambassador to the United Nations.

Dean Barrow
Former "Minister of Everything" in the last UDP government, prominent lawyer and businessman, and the only UDP pol not to lose his seat in the 1998 national elections.

Barry Bowen
Brews Belikin beer, bottles Coca-Cola and owns Chan Chich Lodge and the large farm at Gallon Jug which was once part of the Belize Estate and Produce Company's vast holdings.

Santiago Castillo
Successful business owner and entrepreneur.

Mark Espat
Veteran hotelier who, as Minister of Tourism, is trying to energize this

important segment of the Belize economy.

Ralph Fonseca
The new Minister of Finance is taking a proactive approach to jump-starting the dragging Belize economy.

Stewart Krohn
Krohn and his wife are major stockholders in Belize Channel 5/Great Belize Productions, Belize's leading TV station and most important news source.

Harry Lawrence
Editor of *The Reporter.*

Sharon Matolo
Founder and head of the Belize Zoo, and an outspoken environmentalist.

Said Musa
The PM.

10 National Holidays

January 1: New Year's Day
March 9: Baron Bliss Day
March or April: Easter Friday through Easter Monday
May 1: Labor Day
May 25: Commonwealth Day
September 10: Battle of St. George's Caye Day
September 21: Independence Day
October 12: Columbus Day
November 19: Garifuna Settlement Day
December 25 and 26: Christmas Day and Boxing Day

5 Best Festivals and Events

Belizeans love a party. Here are some of the best:

1 St. George's Caye Day
Parties and celebrations begin September 10 and continue through ...

2 Independence Day
... on September 21.

3 Garifuna Settlement Day
Celebrated November 19 in Dangriga.

4 Carnival
Mardi Gras is a recent arrival in Belize, but it's celebrated in big style with parades, paint "bombs" and, of course, drinking, in Belize City and San Pedro.

5 Costa Maya Festival
Formerly Sea and Air Festival, celebrated with beauty contests, music and dances in San Pedro, late July/early August (dates vary).

Honorable Mention: Crooked Tree Cashew Festival, first week in May

5 Reasons Why Belize Isn't a Major Tourist Destination

1 Belize City
Belize City scares the bejeebers out of the typical North American tourist (white, middle-class). There's a perception among many travelers that Belize City, and ergo the rest of Belize, is unsafe. Belize City needs to clean up it act. Failing that, if Belize built a new international airport in Cayo, Southern Belize or North Ambergris Caye, the number of international visitors would triple within three years.

2 No Clear Brand Identity
The Belize travel brand should stand for a unique travel experience offering reef, ruins and jungle, one that is easily accessible in complete safety and with good value for the price. At present, that image is muddy or, worse, is contradicted by reports of high prices for poor service and other problems.

3 Lack of Great Beaches
For most travelers, the Caribbean equals great beaches. When they learn that beaches in Belize aren't as good as they'd hoped, they (rather foolishly) turn off on Belize, going instead to a tourist trap like Cancun.

4 Lack of Airlift
Belize has only limited, and overpriced, air service from the U.S., and poor to non-existent service from Canada and Europe. It needs more and better service. This is a chicken-and-egg thing, though. Airlines will boost service when there's more demand, and there will be more demand when airlines provide more and cheaper service.

5 Lack of Promotion
Almost everybody in the tourism promotion business outspends Belize. Hotels in Belize are too small to do much international advertising, and in the past Belize's official advertising and PR has been in ineffective dribs and drabs. It's a little better today, but Belize remains woefully under-promoted.

5 Biggest Hotels in Belize

Even the biggest hotels in Belize are no bigger than a roadside Holiday Inn in the U.S. Most Belize hotels have only a few rooms, often as few as two or three. Here are the "large" properties in Belize:

 # 1 Fiesta Inn, Belize City, 118 rooms
(Originally opened as a Ramada, this hotel reportedly is no longer affiliated with the Fiesta Inn chain, but as of this writing was still using the name.)

 # 2 Radisson Fort George, Belize City, 100 rooms

 # 3 Belize Biltmore Plaza, Belize City, 92 rooms

 # 4 Journey's End, Ambergris Caye, 70 rooms

 # 5 Ramon's Village, Ambergris Caye, 60 rooms

10 Most Fanciful Place Names in Belize

Grab a map and take an armchair tour of some of Belize's colorful places.

 # 1 Go-to-Hell Camp
 # 2 Pull Trouser Swamp
 # 3 Never Delay
 # 4 Dog Flea Caye
 # 5 More Tomorrow
 # 6 Good Living Camp
 # 7 Double Head Cabbage
 # 8 Bound to Shine
 # 9 Pork and Doughboy Point
 # 10 Hen and Chicken Cayes

Best Movies Filmed in Belize

Not many movies have been filmed in Belize, but Belizeans are hoping the newly appointed film commissioner, Emory King, can change that.

 # 1 Dogs of War (1981)
Rousing adventure film starring Christopher Walken with Belize doubling for African setting (though Belize gets no screen credit). Great Belize City shots.

 # 2 Mosquito Coast (1986)
Based on the depressing Paul Theroux novel. Harrison Ford plays iconoclastic escapist who ends up playing God.

Planning Your Visit

Photo by Sheila M. Lambert

A young visitor dances with butterflies, on the road through Programme for Belize lands

10 Facts to Know Before You Come

1 Location and Government

Belize (formerly British Honduras) is on the Caribbean Coast of Central America, bordering Mexico and Guatemala. It is a democratic member of the British Commonwealth, with a Westminster-style system with a prime minister, an elected house of representatives and an appointed senate. The current prime minister is Said Musa, a British-educated lawyer of Palestinian and Belize heritage. He heads the People's United Party, which swept national elections in 1998.

2 Size and Population

Belize is about the size of the U.S. state of Massachusetts — 8,866 square miles — with a population of only about 240,000, about as many people as in metro Savannah, Georgia.

3 Language

English is the official language, but Creole, a combination of English, African and other languages, is the *lingua franca.* Spanish is widely spoken. Garifuna and Maya languages also are spoken. Many Belizeans are bi- or tri-lingual.

4 Entry Requirements

You must have a valid passport to enter Belize, with at least six months before expiration, but visas are not required for citizens of the U.S., Canada and the U.K. Entry is granted for up to 30 days, with renewals of up to a total of six months permitted (renewals cost US$12.50 per month.)

5 Money

The Belize currency is the Belize dollar, which is tied to the U.S. dollar at a fixed 2 Belize to 1 U.S. dollar rate. U.S. dollars are accepted everywhere in Belize; Canadian dollars, Mexican pesos and European currencies are not widely accepted. Visa, Master Card and American Express are accepted at many hotels and at some shops and restaurants. ATMs are few.

6 Activities on the Caribbean

Belize offers visitors world-class diving, snorkeling, fishing and other water activities in the Caribbean Sea, around the Belize Barrier Reef, the longest barrier reef in the Western and Northern hemispheres, and on its mainland coast and more than 200 cayes. Boat charters are available. Sea kayaking is a popular sport, and wind surfing is growing in popularity. There is no surfing in Belize.

7 Activities on the Mainland

Belize also offers visitors unspoiled nature on the mainland, with the opportunity to see hundreds of species of birds, rare animals including the jaguar and four other types of cats, the tapir and peccary. Jungle lodges in all price ranges offer comfort and adventure.

8 Maya Ruins

Belize, once the heart of the ancient Maya empire with a population of more than a million people, has Maya ruins everywhere, and at most sites you'll see few other visitors. Caracol, thought to have been larger than Tikal, Lamanai, Xunantunich, Altun Ha and Cahal Pech are the five most popular ruins to visit. Modern Maya comprise a little more than a tenth of the Belize population, mostly concentrated in southern and western Belize.

9 Most Popular Tourist Destinations

The most popular tourist destinations in Belize, in order of visitation, are Ambergris Caye (a resort island about one-half the size of Barbados, with good hotels, restaurants and water sports, but with sand streets and no buildings over three stories), Cayo (Belize's "Wild West" with jungle lodges, Maya ruins, butterfly farms, Mennonites, the gateway to the cool Mountain Pine Ridge and mighty Caracol, and all sorts of outdoor activities including river running and caving), and the Placencia peninsula (a little bit of the South Pacific on the southern mainland, with a growing number of excellent small hotels and restaurants on a long stretch of sandy beach).

10 Off-the-Beaten Path in Belize

Off-the-beaten-path areas of interest to visitors include Corozal Town, a gem of a town close to the Mexico border; Belmopan, Belize's remarkable (and remarkably small) capital; Punta Gorda, Belize's southern outpost and icon for the "real Belize"; Caye Caulker, a budget version of Ambergris Caye but with its own style; the Shipstern/Sarteneja peninsula, where doing nothing is a way of life; Hopkins/Sittee Point, what Placencia was just a few years ago, and friendly as heck; Gales Point, hauntingly beautiful; rural Orange Walk District, home to several top jungle lodges, hundreds of thousands of acres of unspoiled nature; Crooked Tree, the birding haven; Dangriga, jumping off point for many cayes and the center of Belize's Garifuna culture; the Maya Mountains, rugged and little explored in modern times; and the offshore cayes and atolls, where life is slow and diving is fantastic.

10 Top Destinations for Visitors

1 Ambergris Caye

Beginning in the early 1950s, and accelerating beginning in the 1970s and 80s, this was the first area of Belize to develop for tourism. It remains the most popular destination in the country. And for good reason. It offers a variety of sand and sea activities, a spectrum of hotel rooms from budget to deluxe, good restaurants, and the option of land tours. While tourism is the leading activity and considerable development has occurred, the streets are still sand, golf carts are still the main type of transportation, and no building is over three stories. There are no big cruise ships vomiting day trippers, as on many Caribbean islands. Visitors feel safe and comfortable here. Snorkeling (from a boat) is excellent, and the recreational diving is good. *You'll love it here if you like a laid-back resort atmosphere without too much commercialization.*

2 Cayo District

About 20 years ago, the first small jungle lodges began operation around San Ignacio. Now, there is a flourishing mix of hotels, cottages and jungle lodges near San Ignacio and in the Mountain Pine Ridge, along with a lot of natural attractions and outdoor activities — canoeing, caving, hiking, horseback riding, to name a few. The country's most accessible Maya ruins are here, as well as Caracol, in its heyday in the Classic Period a larger city-state than Tikal. And speaking of Tikal, Cayo is the Belize gateway to that astounding site. For many visitors, Cayo is the turf in the classic Belize surf 'n turf. Betwixt Belize City and San Ignacio, Belmopan is the down-sized capital of Belize, but the attractions are not in the capital itself but in the countryside. The Belize Zoo is here, as are several excellent jungle lodges. Along the scenic Hummingbird Highway and nearby are barely explored caves, wild rivers and national park areas. *You'll love it here if you like outdoor activities and an uncrowded "Wild West" atmosphere.*

3 Placencia

In recent years, the Placencia peninsula has been undergoing a boom (a Belize-style boom, anyway) with the development of about a dozen new small beach resorts and new restaurants, including excellent Italian and French ones, adding to the existing inventory of small high-quality inns and budget hotels. Building lots have been sold by the score, to foreigners who think they'd someday like to live by the sea. At the same time, the peninsula hasn't changed that much: Seine Bight is still a very poor Garifuna village, Placencia, a Creole village, still has its plank sidewalk, and the largest grocery is the size of your living room. The beach is still a pleasant, sometimes garbage-strewn long narrow stretch of sand. The reef is almost 20 miles offshore here, but there are closer cayes for good snorkeling. *You'll love it here if you want a little bit of the South Pacific in Central America.*

4 Caye Caulker

Caulker slowly is going up-market, but it remains mostly a budget version of Ambergris Caye, with small locally owned hotels and modest restaurants. Some think the island is a little funky; others say it's just laid-back. Diving and snorkeling are similar to Ambergris Caye. *You'll love it here if you like a small, easy-going island with budget prices.*

5 Remote Cayes

When romantics dream about the Caribbean, with coco palms swaying in the tradewinds and the reef just steps off the sandy shore, the remote cayes are what they're dreaming of. Belize has more than 200 islands in the sea. Almost all of them are tiny, most are unpopulated, and many are incredibly beautiful, with sandbanks backing up to gin-clear water. A few, around Belize's three atolls, are as South Pacific as you can get in this hemisphere. So what's the catch? Why do visitors to remote cayes number only a few thousand a year? Because they *are* remote and small and difficult to get to. Airstrips are rare; boat trips out to them are expensive and may involve puking your guts out in that gin-clear water. With exceptions of a few expensive dive resorts, accommodations are mostly basic, with limited or non-existent running water and electricity. Tropical storms and hurricanes periodically destroy what accommodations there are. There are few places to eat, and no shops. But for those who want to get away to a deserted tropical island, a visit to South Water, Little Water, Northeast, Ranguana or other remote caye could be the experience of a lifetime. *You'll love it if all you want is sun, sand and sea.*

6 Corozal Town Area

Most visitors see Corozal only as an overnight stop on the road from the Yucatán to the Belize cayes or Cayo, but Corozal in fact is one of the undiscovered jewels of Belize, with friendly folks and low prices on the beautiful Bay of Chetumal. There's not a lot to do, but it's a great place to do it. *You'll love it, if you want to slow down and enjoy a Mexican-Belizean experience.*

7 Belize City and Belize District

Belize City's reputation (far worse than the reality) frightens most North American tourists, which is too bad, because Belize City offers a side of Belize that you don't get to see elsewhere. It's a busy, bustling and colorful port city with excellent restaurants and pleasant hotels. Nearby is a wealth of interesting things to see, including the Community Baboon Sanctuary, Crooked Tree Wildlife Sanctuary and Altun Ha. *You'll love it if you don't bring misconceptions in your luggage.*

8 Hopkins Area

This is what Placencia was like just a decade or so ago. Expats are moving in to Hopkins, a friendly Garifuna village that got telephones only a couple of years ago, and to "real estate subdivisions" nearby. New small seaside hotels are going up in Hopkins and Sittee Point. Although at times the sand flies can eat you alive here, you can get in some excellent fishing and beach time, with day trips to nearby Cockscomb and boat trips to the reef. *You'll love it if Placencia is too developed for you.*

9 Punta Gorda

Belize tourism promoters refer to this as Belize's outpost. It's certainly that, the jumping off point for unspoiled Maya villages and for onward travel to Guatemala and Honduras. At present, few tourists venture this far south. Over the next few years, however, as the Southern Highway resurfacing is completed and the road is (possibly) extended into Guatemala, this area will take off — again, by Belizean standards and at least in the dry season — in tourism development. Come see it now. *You'll love it if you want an ends-of-the-earth ambiance.*

10 Rural Orange Walk District

Farms, jungle and wildlife are about all you'll find here. Orange Walk Town itself is not of much appeal to visitors, but once you're away from town, this is authentic Belize. Several of Belize's best jungle lodges are located here. *You'll love it if you'd be happier living in 1940 than today.*

5 Do-able Itineraries for Belize

Although you can base in one area or island and do day trips to other areas, most visitors staying more than a few days find it easier and cheaper to base themselves in two or more areas.

If you have less than a week:
Unless you are a Type A traveler, limit your visit to one easily accessible area, with good options being either Ambergris Caye or the Placencia peninsula for sun and sea, or Cayo District for Maya ruins, bush and wildlife.

If you have 7 days:
Divide your trip into a mainland and sea segment:
Ambergris Caye or Placencia: 3 days
Cayo: 4 days

If you have 10 days:
Stay longer in two areas, or visit three different places:
Ambergris Caye: 3 days
Placencia or Hopkins area or a remote caye: 3 days
Cayo or rural Orange Walk: 4 days

If you have 14 days:
Add either Toledo or Corozal/Orange Walk district.

If you have 21 days:
In three weeks, you can see at least the highlights of what Belize has to offer, although four weeks would be better. A recommended division:

Ambergris Caye or Caye Caulker: 4 days
Remote caye: 4 days
Placencia or Hopkins: 3 days
Cayo/Mountain Pine Ridge/Tikal: 4 days
Punta Gorda: 2 days
Corozal/Orange Walk districts: 3 days
Belize City and Belize District: 1 day

Ideal Unlimited Itinerary

If you have plenty of time and plenty of money, here's the ideal itinerary for Belize:

Days 1-7: Decompress on Ambergris Caye
Fly into the international airport, then hop a 20-minute flight to San Pedro, for a week of relaxation, sun and getting into the pace of Belize. Do day sails to Caye Caulker and Half Moon Caye/Blue Hole.

Days 8-13: Explore Northern Belize
Return to Belize City, pick up a rental car, and head up the Northern Highway. Explore Crooked Tree, Community Baboon Sanctuary, Altun Ha, Orange Walk Town, Corozal Town and the Sarteneja peninsula.

Days 14-19: Wildlife Spotting in Orange Walk District
Drive to Gallon Jug and Lamanai for wildlife spotting, birding and Maya ruin trips. Stay at top jungle lodges.

Days 20-22: Capital, My Dear Fellow
Drive to Belmopan, seeing the capital, Belize Zoo, Guanacaste park and other sites, staying at a jungle lodge near Belmopan.

Days 23-27: Discover Cayo
Drive to Cayo. Stay at one of the cottage colonies or jungle lodges. Explore San Ignacio town, ruins of Cahal Pech, Xunantunich, El Pilar, Che Chem Ha. Try horseback riding, caving, rivering. Visit Mennonite areas.

Days 28-30: Tikal
Visit Tikal, staying near the ruins.

Days 31-34: Mountain Pine Ridge
Drive into the reserve, staying at a good lodge. Hike, visit waterfalls, caves. Tour Caracol.

Days 35-40: Garifuna Days
Drive down the beautiful Hummingbird Highway, with stops at Five Blues and Blue Hole parks. Spend a few nights in Dangriga and Hopkins, with side trips to Gales Point, Cockscomb Jaguar Preserve, and Red Bank to see the scarlet macaws.

Days 41-46: Placencia
Relax on the Placencia peninsula, dive or snorkel the southern reef and cayes, with side trips to Monkey River.

Days 47-52: Toledo

Drive to PG and explore Belize's southern outpost. Overnight in Maya villages. Do a short trip to Puerto Barrios/Livingston, Guatemala.

Days 52-54: Return to Belize City
By now you're mellow enough to enjoy Belize City. Explore this hub of Creole culture.

Days 55-65: Remote Cayes and Atolls
Get out in the Caribbean, with a long visit to an atoll such as Lighthouse and/or or to one or more of the small cayes such as South Water. Remember, you'll need at least 24 hours after your last dive before you can fly out.

10 Things to Pack for Your Trip

Time-worn advice for travelers is to pack half the clothes and twice the money you think you'll need.

1 Extra swimsuits
At least two — let one dry while you're wearing the other. On the cayes or coast, you'll live in your swimsuit.

2 Light-weight cotton clothes and comfortable shoes
Tee-shirts, shorts, loose-fitting slacks and shirts, light boots or walking shoes, plus a pair of sandals or canvas shoes for the beach.

3 Maps, guidebooks and reading material
If available at all in Belize, these will cost more than back home and likely will be old editions. Although some hotels have libraries for guests, Belize has no large bookstores and finding the latest John Grisham novel may prove impossible.

4 Extra film
Film is widely available in Belize, but it costs two to three times more than at Wal-Mart back home.

5 Baggies and duct tape
Zip-lock or similar plastic bags in various sizes are useful for storing everything from wet socks to special seashells. Duct tape fixes anything.

6 Small flashlight and Swiss Army-style knife
You'll want to be able to spot that small creature scurrying across the ceiling in the middle of the night. A small pocket knife with several tools always comes in handy.

7 Hat or cap and dark sunglasses
A well-fitting hat or cap that will stay on in the wind is a true friend to your

head. Dark sunglasses are a must for glare on the water.

8 Basic health kit
In a plastic bag, pack your prescription medicines, plus aspirin, insect spray with up to 30% DEET, sunscreen, Pepto, bandages, sun-burn lotion, seasick pills and other over-the-counter medicines you think you'll need.

9 Favorite snacks
Grocery stores in Belize City and elsewhere are well-stocked but may not have your favorite snacks. We usually bring our own parmesan Goldfish. Avoid bringing chocolate or other items that melt in tropical temps.

10 Battery-operated radio
A small shortwave/FM/AM radio is handy to have at hand, especially in hurricane season or when in remote jungle areas.

5 Things NOT to Bring
(Besides guns and drugs, of course.)

1 Suits, ties or dress clothes of any kind
Casual clothes, mainly shorts and open-collar shirts, or a light dress, are all you'll need for most activities in Belize. You'll be comfortable in Belize's fanciest restaurants in a shirt and slacks. Even the Prime Minister wears a guayaberra or a white dress shirt with open collar.

2 Jewelry
Only street thieves will be impressed with your diamonds and gold.

3 Leather items
High humidity, sweat and salt water do a number on leather. Where possible, canvas is better.

4 Spear guns
If customs sees your spear guns, they'll likely confiscate them.

5 A grumpy attitude
Be happy!

10 Best Belize Guidebooks

1 *Rough Guide to Belize,* by Peter Eltringham, Rough Guides/Penguin, 1999
Solid, reliable research and especially good coverage of less-expensive options mark this guidebook, one in a wonderful series put out by self-described

"English eccentrics." Peter Eltringham first came to Belize with the Royal Air Force and has lived in Guatemala and Belize.

 # 2 *Belize Handbook,* **by Chicki Mallan, 4th ed., Moon Publications, 1998**
This Moon guide, with updating by Patti Lange, is, like most in the terrific Moon series, well organized, thoughtfully designed and absolutely packed with valuable information.

 # 3 *Belize, Adventures in Nature,* **by Richard Mahler, 2nd ed., John Muir, 1999**
Excellent on the natural side of Belize. Refreshingly different from other guides.

 # 4 *The EcoTraveller's Wildlife Guide to Belize and Northern Guatemala,* **by Les Beletsky, Academic Press, 1999**
New guide for birders and visitors interested in nature has incredible color plates of Belize birds, reptiles, mammals and fish.

 # 5 *Explore Belize,* **by Harry Pariser, 4th ed., Hunter Publications, 1998**
New edition of what was *Adventure Guide to Belize.* Lots of detail, eco-oriented

 # 6 *Insight Guides Belize,* **Tony Perrottet, (editor), 2nd ed., Houghton-Mifflin, 1997**
Gorgeous, unbeatable photos and good historical information. It's best for background reading.

 # 7 *Fodor's Belize & Guatemala,* **Christine Cipriani (editor), Fodor's Travel Publications, 1998**
The Belize section is thin but well-informed. Easy-to-use format.

 # 8 *Destination Belize,* **Ulrich Communications for BTIA**
Technically an annual magazine rather than a guidebook, "the official visitor magazine of the Belize Tourism Industry Association" provides a good overview for the first-time visitor to Belize, though nary a negative word is heard.

 # 9 *Guatemala, Belize & Yucatán, La Ruta Maya,* **by Tom Brosnahan and Nancy Keller, 3rd ed., Lonely Planet, 1997**
Superb information on Maya sites; the update is spotty.

 # 10 *Diving & Snorkeling Belize,* **by Franz O. Meyer, 2nd. ed., Lonely Planet, 1998**
The best guide to snorkel and dive sites in and around the atolls and northern

cayes and reef; weak on coverage of everything else, and little on the southern cayes and reef.

Honorable Mention:
Guide to Belize, by Alex Bradbury, 2nd ed., Bradt/Globe Pequot 1996
Belize, by Carlos Soldevila, Ulysses Travel Publications, 1998

5 Best Belize Maps

In most cases, you're better off buying your Belize map before you get to Belize.

1 *Belize Traveller's Map,* ITMB
This 350,000:1-scale map, lasted updated in 1998, is the best available general map of Belize.

2 *Emory King's Driver's Guide to Beautiful Belize*
More of a mile-by-mile driver's guide than a map, and in its 11th edition in 1999, this is a must-have if you're traveling around Belize by car or bus. We wish it had maps of Ambergris and Caulker.

3 Topographical Map of Belize, British Ordnance Survey
This two-sheet topo map at 250,000:1-scale was last revised in 1990-91 so it's not as up-to-date as it could be, but it looks nice on your wall. The reverse side has helpful maps of Belize City and all the towns.

4 Ordnance Survey Area Maps
Belize has been divided into 44 sections and mapped at 50,000:1-scale by the British Ordnance Survey. Unfortunately, some of these maps were done years ago and are much out-of-date.

5 *Savanna's Bohemian Guide to Ambergris Caye*
This advertising map, from 1995, provides a three-dimensional view of Ambergris Caye and many of its hotels and businesses. A similar map is available to Cayo.

10 Best Belize Web Sites

Possibly no destination in the world — and certainly no other country the size of Belize — has so many informative and interesting Web sites as Belize. In fact, Belize may soon have more Web home pages than actual homes ... or tourists. Out of fairness, we didn't include our own Web sites at www.turq.com/belizefirst/ or www.turq.com/equator/, which are ad-free.

1 Belize by Naturalight (www.belizenet.com)
Tony Rath has put together a terrific site, with stunning graphics, beautiful photos (but what else would you expect from one of the Caribbean Coast's premier shooters?) and tons of good information. Well-managed newsgroup, requiring preregistration.

2 Ambergris Caye (www.ambergriscaye.com)
Everything you always wanted to know about San Pedro. Excellent!

3 Channel 5/Great Belize Productions (www.channel5belize.com)
Excellent source of reliable Belize news, presented daily Monday - Friday.

4 You Better Belize It (www.belizeit.com)
Something of a mishmash of information and promotion, but lively and with frequent visits by Belizeans living outside Belize.   Recently purchased by Tony Rath of Belize by Naturalight, who says he plans to upgrade the site.

5 Cayo On-Line (www.belizex.com)
Useful site devoted to Cayo District.

6 *San Pedro Sun* (www.ambergriscaye.com/sanpedrosun/)
Like the newspaper, this home page is friendly, chatty, informative, and upbeat.

7 Belize Zoo (www.belizezoo.org)
Delightful site about the "best little zoo in the world" with terrific animal photos, including Quick Time movies

8 Chat 'Bout Belize (www.chatboutbelize.com)
Ambitious site, focused on Belizeans and home and abroad.

9 Belizean CyberWeb (www.belizeanweb.com)
Neil Fraser's collection of old British Honduras photos is posted here.

10 (tie) Belize Audubon Society (www.belizeaudubon.org)
Wonderful site from Belize's premier conservation group. Another tremendous design job by the Belize by Naturalight folks.

10 (tie) Placencia (www.placencia.com)
Useful for trip planning.

10 (tie) Corozal (www.corozal.com)
Good effort, mostly by Corozal Community College and Corozal Junior College staff and students.

 # 10 (tie) Belize On-Line (www.belize.com)
Belizean Manolo Romero and his U.S. partners were early pioneers of the use of the Web to promote Belize. Unfortunately the site was neglected, although Romero now runs it alone and may make improvements.

5 Sources of Free Information on Belize

In addition to these sources of information subscribers to BELIZE FIRST may e-mail us (BZEFIRST@aol.com) and we will try to answer all questions individually within 48 hours.

 # 1 Internet
The Internet offers tens of thousands of pages of free information on Belize. Remember, though, that much of what you see on the Web is paid advertising or electronic brochures. *Caveat emptor.* Belize forums and newsgroups, especially on Belize by Naturalight, AmbergrisCaye.com and You Better Belize It Web sites, and on the Belize section of the AOL travel forum, are a good source of usually candid first-person advice about Belize. The Belize Culture mailing list is also excellent, though this is not a tourism-oriented list. Subscribe by e-mailing bz-culture-request@psg.com the word "subscribe".

 # 2 Belize Tourist Board
The BTB has closed, for reasons unknown, its New York office, but you can still dial toll-free in the U.S., 800-624-0686, and the phone will be answered in Belize City. E-mail btb@btl.net, Web www.belizenet.com.

 # 3 Embassy of the United States in Belize
The U.S. Embassy is at 29 Gabourel Lane, Belize City, tel. 501-2-77161, fax 2-30802. Hours are 8 a.m. to noon and 1 to 4 p.m. Monday-Friday. The current U.S.Ambassador is Carolyn Curiel. E-mail embbelize@belizwpoa.us-state.gov. The embassy's Web site at www.usemb-belize.gov/ provides some useful information.

 # 4 Belize Tourism Industry Association
Organization of hotels and tourism operators sponsors an annual magazine on Belize called *Destination Belize,* sold by the Belize Tourism Board (see above). Tel. 501-2-72464 in Belize City.

 # 5 Embassy of Belize in the United States
2535 Massachusetts Ave., Washington, DC 20008, tel. 202-232-9636. Although the staff here are overworked and underpaid, they may be able to provide some help on official matters including living/retiring in Belize.

5 Knowledgeable Tour Operators

These operators provide a wide variety of guided tour and adventure trips to Belize and other destinations.

(Listed alphabetically)

International Expeditions, Helena, Alabama
Large, well-experienced operator.

International Zoological Expeditions, Sherborn, Massachusetts
IZE offers trips to its cabins on Long Caye and South Water Caye, and to its rain forest cabins at Blue Creek in Toledo District.

Island Expeditions, Vancouver, British Columbia, Canada
Specializes in sea and river kayaking trips.

Magnum Belize, Detroit Lakes, Minnesota
Mainly books hotel and air packages to Belize.

Slickrock Adventures, Moab, Utah
Sea kayaking and river and jungle trips in Belize and elsewhere.

Best Airlines from U.S. to Belize

Only three airlines currently have service to Belize from the U.S. Delta may begin service soon. Commuters also provide service from Mexico, Guatemala and Honduras. At present, there is no direct or non-stop service to Belize from Canada or Europe, except the occasional charter.

1 Continental
Although all airlines can have bad days, we've found Continental, with its twice-daily non-stop Houston-Belize City service, usually to be the best of the bunch in terms of friendliness and clean, reasonably comfortable equipment.

2 (tie) American
Highly professional service, both in the U.S. and in Belize.

3 (tie) TACA
TACA has been serving Belize for more than 60 years. Grupo Taca is now an alliance of several Central American airlines including Aviateca, Lacsa, Nica, TACA and TACA de Honduras, with the main hub and headquarters in San Salvador. We've always found TACA's service, food and free beverages above average, though coach seating on the 737s is really jammed. But Belizeans were unhappy when TACA discontinued non-stop Miam-Belize

service in the spring of 1999. Thanks to the efforts of the Belize Tourism Board, non-stop 737 service resumed in June 1999, with continuing service to Flores (Tikal) and Guatemala City. TACA also has non-stops from Houston.

Best Belize Airlines

There are only two, and we haven't found much difference between them in terms of price, service, safety or comfort.

1 (tie) Tropic Air
John Grief Sr., operator with wife Celi, of the San Pedro Holiday Hotel, pioneered air travel on Ambergris Caye and now flies a fleet of Cessna Caravans and other equipment serving Belize City (international and municipal airports), San Pedro, Caye Caulker, Dangriga, Punta Gorda, Placencia, Corozal and Flores, Guatemala. It also offers charter service.

1 (tie) Maya Island Air
Based on Ambergris Caye, Maya Island hubs in Belize City (municipal and international airports) and has about 140 flights a day serving the same markets as Tropic Air — Belize City, San Pedro, Caye Caulker, Dangriga, Punta Gorda, Placencia, Corozal and Flores, Guatemala. Charter service also available.

5 Belize Bus Lines

Several bus lines serve Belize. Most concentrate on routes to one or two areas. Here are some of the larger lines. Most Belize buses are converted from old U.S. school buses or Greyhound-style buses.

(Listed alphabetically)
Batty
Runs the Northern and Western Highways; operates several deluxe coaches.

James
Belize City south.

Novelos
Western Highway.

Venus
Operates on the Northern Highway.

Z-Line
Operates mostly from Belize City south to Punta Gorda.

5 Health Problems to Watch Out For

Belize generally has fairly high standards of health and hygiene. That's one of the big differences in a trip to Belize and one to Mexico. But Belize is a developing semi-tropical country, with some of the health concerns common to this type of destination. The risk of cholera and typhoid, serious diseases elsewhere in the region, is considered low in Belize. Rabies is present, but rarely affects travelers. Belize has a shortage of doctors, especially in rural areas, but treatment is available, by generally well-trained physicians, in Belize City, on Ambergris Caye and in larger towns such as Dangriga and San Ignacio. Check with the U.S. Embassy in Belize for a list of recommended physicians. Pharmacies, mainly in Belize City, stock most commonly prescribed drugs, but savvy travelers will bring all medicines they routinely take. For the big picture, check with the Centers for Disease Control in Atlanta (www.cdc.org, tel. 800-311-3435 or 404-639-3311) or your local physician.

1 Sunburn
This is the most common problem for fair-skinned travelers. Belize is closer to the equator than the U.S., Canada or Europe, and the sun is far more intense. Use sunscreen and plenty of it. Snorkel in a tee-shirt.

2 Stomach Upsets
You can drink the water in most areas of Belize (ask locally if you're not sure), and even street food is usually safe, but that doesn't mean you won't get Belize Belly. The local microbes may be just different enough from those back home to give your system fits. Another culprit is the combination of hot sun and too many Belikins. If you have a nervous tummy, a daily dose of Pepto usually will help prevent any problems. If you get an upset, avoid medicines which "plug" you up; instead, rest, eat bland foods lightly (papaya is helpful to some) and drink plenty of fluids. If problems continue, see a doctor.

3 Sand Fly Bites
Some people aren't much bothered by no-see-ums. Some are. Sand flies are common in mangrove swamp areas and in the sand in some areas, notably the Hopkins area, Caye Caulker and Placencia. Quite a few travelers go home with ugly bites which don't seem to heal. If that happens to you, see your doctor who can prescribe an ointment which usually will quickly take care of the bites.

4 Malaria
Ask a Belize resident about malaria, and you'll often get the response, "I've lived here for 17 years, I don't take anything, and I never got malaria." With mosquito eradication programs in place in Belize, malaria is much less of a problem now than it was even as late as the 1980s. But the fact is that there

are still several thousand cases of malaria reported in Belize every year, mainly in the south and in remote areas of the north and west. Cases of malaria are rare in populated areas such as Belize City and on the cayes. Most travelers to these areas don't take any special precautions. Note, however, that the CDC states there is malaria risk everywhere in Belize except in Belize District. If you're going to the far south or to remote jungle areas, certainly it's better to be safe than sorry. Cover up at times, such as the early evening, when the *Anopheles* mosquito is active, use an insect repellent with DEET, and consider taking chloroquine (trade name Aralen), generally considered a safe and effective prophylaxsis for areas where strains are not chloroquine-resistant. Check with the CDC for the latest information, or see your doctor.

5 Dengue Fever

Dengue fever is not common in Belize, but it does occur in the region — it has been widespread in the Yucatán — and sometimes occurs in Belize, especially during and just after the rainy season. Symptoms of the types of dengue found in Belize are similar to that of the flu. At present, there is no preventive medicine. Avoid getting bitten by the *Aedes aegypti* mosquito, which, unlike the mosquito which transmits malaria, is often found indoors in urban areas and is active during the day, with prime feeding times being the morning and late afternoon. If you get it, rest and take acetaminophen (Tylenol and other brands), not aspirin.

Dishonorable Mention: Chagas' disease, or the "kissing bug" disease, transmitted by a bug which in Belize is occasionally present in the thatch roofs of poorly maintained structures and which drops down to bite and infect its victim. Chagas' disease can be effectively treated with drugs, but if left untreated it can permanently damage the heart. There is very, very slight risk of filariasis, leishmaniasis and onchocerciasis (look'em up) in Belize.

5 Sticks and Pills to Consider

The only required inoculation to visit Belize is for yellow fever, and that is only if you're coming from an infected area such as Sub-Saharan Africa or parts of South America including Venezuela, Colombia and Brazil. See your doc or listen to the CDC's advice, but experienced travelers to Belize often recommend the following preventative sticks and pills.

1 Boosters for Tetanus, Diphtheria and Measles

Keep your shots up-to-date.

2 Hepatitis A

Sticks for long-term protection against Hep A are now available. These are good insurance for any traveler.

3 Hepatitis B
Especially if you are staying for long periods or think you might have sexual contact or contact with blood.

4 Chloroquine for Malaria
This once-weekly tab, which must be taken one week before arrival, weekly during the trip, and then for four weeks following, is considered a safe prophylaxsis for the type of malaria present in parts of Belize; side effects are not significant for most people. Young children may find the pill difficult to take.

5 Typhoid
Typhoid fever is not usually a problem in Belize, but occasional limited outbreaks do occur in Belize and, more commonly, in neighboring countries. Check before you go to see current status. Vaccines for typhoid are not completely effective, so the best prevention is to avoid risky food and drink.

5 Ways to Get Medical Care in Belize

Belize has a mixed medical system. Most Belizeans get low-cost or free care at a system of government-run hospitals and clinics around the country. In addition, there are doctors with private practices who offer services for fee. Most doctors in Belize are foreign-born and trained. The problem is that there are too few of them. There are fewer than 100 physicians in all of Belize, although these are supplemented by periodic visits by teams of doctors from Cuba, the U.S., Canada and other countries. Belize has a nursing school in Belize City, along with two offshore medical schools, St. Matthews in San Pedro and Belize Medical School in Belize City. The offshore schools offer training for foreign students unable to get into U.S. medical schools. If you become ill in Belize, here are the options you have:

Get emergency care at a local public hospital or clinic
Besides Karl Heusner Memorial Hospital and a variety of clinics in Belize City, there are district hospitals in Corozal Town, Orange Walk Town, Belmopan, San Ignacio, Dangriga and Punta Gorda. Areas without clinics or a resident doctor may have a nurse or visiting doctor. The standard of facilities varies; Dangriga Hospital is new and Karl Heusner is nearly so, but some other hospitals and clinics are old and outmoded. Care also varies, depending on availability of equipment and supplies and on the skills of doctors and nurses in attendance. Due to heavy demand, you may have to wait a long while for someone to see you. Costs for care are much lower than for comparable care in the U.S. A private volunteer group, Wings of Hope, transports emergency cases by air to the nearest hospital; if you can afford to pay, you'll have make

reimbursement for transportation.

Visit a private physician or clinic
In Belize City and on Ambergris Caye, and to a lesser degree in San Ignacio and Corozal Town and in other towns, there are private physicians who can treat you much as does your primary care physician back home. Belize City also has a number of dentists. A visit to a doctor will cost about US$15, plus any medicines prescribed. Check with your country's embassy in Belize for a list of physicians. Costs for most types of care will be lower than in the U.S., and care may be good although not always up to the standards you expect.

Go to Chetumal
Chetumal, the capital of the state of Yucatán and just north of Corozal Town, has more than twice the population of Belize's largest city, Belize City. It has private physicians and clinics which, in many cases, can provide high-quality care at a much lower price than care in the U.S. or in Belize. Dental care in Chetumal also is very inexpensive. For care not available in Chetumal, another option is Guatemala City, the largest city in Central America. Even in colonial days, many Belizeans flew to Guatemala City for care.

Go to the U.S.
For a serious illness such as a heart attack, you may want to do what wealthy Belizeans do — go to Houston, Miami or elsewhere in the U.S. Obviously, the cost of emergency medical flights to the U.S. is high — the charge may run to tens of thousands of dollars. Some travel insurance and even some platinum credit cards may pay for emergency medical evacuation.

See a bush doctor
Belize has a rich tradition of natural and herbal medicine. The most famous, Don Eligio Panti, died in 1996 at well over age 100. Ask locally for recommendations on the nearest bush doctor or snake doctor. The best of them combine natural healing with an instinct for when to direct patients to a local clinic or hospital.

Best Times to Visit

Anytime is a good time to visit, but here are the "best times" for different activities and budgets:

Best time for underwater visibility: April-June
Late spring and early summer offer the best water viz.

Best time for lowest hotel prices: After Easter to Thanksgiving
Exact dates vary by hotel.

Best time to visit the far south: February-May
It's usually dry in Toledo during these months.

Best time to visit Cayo: July-March
After the rains come, it cools down in Cayo.

Best time to visit Mountain Pine Ridge: July-November
Late spring can be hot and dry, and winter months can be surprisingly chilly.

Best time to visit Placencia: January-May
Sunny with not too much rain, though Northers can chill things in January and February.

Best time to visit cayes: December-June
Sunny with not too much rain; Northers blow through occasionally December-February.

Best time to avoid tourists: September
September is the slowest month of the year for tourism.

5 Driest Months of the Year

Although rainfall varies in different parts of the country, and from year to year, on average the following are the months with the least rain.

 # 1 April
At the height of the "dry season," rain is rare anywhere in Belize.

 # 2 March
Less than 2" of rain in most areas of Belize.

 # 3 February
Ditto.

 # 4 January
But it's usually still wet in January in the far south.

 # 5 May
The last month before the official start of the hurricane season and the usual start of seasonal rains in much of Belize.

Great Honeymoon Ideas

Belize is a popular honeymoon spot. With some prior planning, visitors even get married in Belize. Here, in no particular order, are our suggestions for great honeymoon destinations in Belize.

For Soft Adventure in the Jungle
Here are four jungle lodges where you can enjoy nature with creature comforts and privacy:
• **Chan Chich Lodge,** Orange Walk District. In the middle of the bush, with cut trails for easy jungle access and good local guides to share their knowledge with you. Cabañas are single units for privacy. Very safe, very good.
• **Lamanai Outpost Lodge,** Orange Walk District. Beautiful setting on the New River Lagoon near Lamanai ruins. Take a spotlight nature tour at night. Thatch cabañas aren't fancy but are well-designed and private.
• **Jaguar Paw,** Belmopan Area. Ride the river and explore caves by day, enjoy good food and air conditioned comfort by night.
• **Ek' Tun,** near San Ignacio. Two deluxe cabins, each private, in a lush jungle setting, with excellent food.

For Luxury
For a sybaritic honeymoon, consider one of these options:
• Villa units at **Blancaneaux,** Mountain Pine Ridge. You'll live like a movie star at Francis Ford Coppola's place. Swim in the river, visit nearby waterfalls, tour the ancient city of Caracol.
• Beachfront owners' villas at **Victoria House,** Ambergris Caye. Luxurious designer villas directly on the water.
• Condo units at **Villas at Banyan Bay, The Palms** or **Banana Beach,** Ambergris Caye. Lots of space, and units at Banana Beach and Banyan Bay have whirlpools.
• **Cayo Espanto,** a small private island near Ambergris Caye, has individual houses with pools.

Budget Honeymoon
• Stay in a tent at a "safari" camp at **Chaa Creek** near San Ignacio.
• Honeymoon in a "tree house" at **Parrot's Nest** near San Ignacio.
• Rough it (a little) on the reef in a cabin on Tobacco, Ranguana, South Water, Long or other small caye.
• Camp at Cockscomb Preserve — common kitchens are available to cook your own meals.
• Enjoy an island on a budget with a spic 'n span room at **Tree Tops Hotel, Chocolate's** or **Tom's Hotel,** Caye Caulker.

Kickback and Relax Honeymoon
For a low key, no-pressure honeymoon, try one of these:
• Enjoy a beautiful tropical island at **Pelican Beach Resort's** cottages on South Water Caye.
• Relax, snorkel and doze at **Little Water Caye.**

- Enjoy a taste of the South Pacific at a beach cabaña at **Turtle Inn,** Placencia.
- Treat yourself to a private cabaña at **Lighthouse Reef Resort.**
- Do a beach holiday in one of the three cabañas at **Beaches and Dreams,** Sittee Point.

Get Away from It All
- Charter a sailboat and visit your choice of more than 200 islands in the Caribbean off the coast of Belize (see 5 Boat Charters, page 77).
- Rent your own private island — French Louis Caye is one that's available for around US$150 a day. It has a wooden house, snorkeling right off the beach, and no mosquitoes. (Reserve through **Kitty's,** Placencia.)

5 Things to Know about Marrying in Belize

Marriages in Belize are conducted in the tradition of British common law and are recognized world-wide.

1 Residency
You must be in Belize for three days before you can apply for a license.

2 Marriage License and Blood Test
Marriage licenses can be obtained in Belize City at the General Registry office or Belmopan at the Solicitor General's office, during normal working hours. Cost US$100. No blood test is needed; parental consent not needed if over 18.

3 Paperwork
You need proof of citizenship. A valid passport will do, or a certified copy of birth certificate, which includes father's name, signed by a notary public. Proof of divorce needed if applicable — original or certified copy of divorce decree. If widowed, you'll need a copy of the partner's death decree.

4 Ceremony
A Justice of the Peace can conduct the ceremony at a magistrate's office; in Belize City, the Registrar General can conduct the ceremony at the Registry office. If you prefer a religious ceremony, most ministers in Belize can perform the ceremony at a church or at a hotel or private home.

5 Assistance
Resort hotels on Ambergris Caye, in Placencia, Cayo and elsewhere can assist with wedding details, including help with obtaining a minister or JP and getting the license, if you are staying at the hotel. Some Belize tour operators also provide wedding assistance.

Belize Travel Tips

Photo by Marty Casado

Soft breezes through the coco palms, with the ridiculously blue
Caribbean behind them, await you in Belize

10 Best Things to Do with Kids

Belize is best for kids old enough to appreciate nature and to entertain themselves outdoors. There are no fast-food restaurants, malls or video game parlors in Belize, but many hotels in Belize City, San Pedro and a few other places do offer cable TV with all the U.S. channels.

1 Visit the Belize Zoo
Hands down, this is Belize's favorite place for kids of all ages.

2 Beach it
All over Belize, you'll see local kids swimming off piers and beaches. Belize's beaches may not be as wide and sandy as some, but kids don't mind. They'll have a ton of fun.

3 Hang out with Belizean kids
About two-thirds of Belizeans are under age 21, so kids are everywhere.

4 Go snorkeling
Kids as young as 5 or 6 can enjoy the wonders of undersea life, but don't push them too fast. If you're with a guide, ask for water wings or a life jacket for the little ones, as some currents through the reef are strong.

5 Climb a Maya ruin
Young'uns go where adults are too tired to tread — they love running up and down the temples and other structures at Altun Ha, Xunantunich, Lamanai and elsewhere. Kids may not think much of the history, but they'll enjoy the exercise.

6 Take a guided nature hike
Most Belize guides are highly knowledgeable about wildlife and flora. They'll open the eyes of your kids to all kinds of natural wonders. Tarantulas, crocs, snakes, wee-wee ants and monkeys seem to hold more appeal than bird for kids. Young people seem especially to enjoy seeing and hearing the howler monkeys — there are troops at Community Baboon Sanctuary, at Lamanai, in Cayo, around Monkey River and elsewhere.

7 Hit the river
Most kids will get a kick out of swimming or tubing in one of Belize's many rivers. Resorts, lodges and tour operators offer river trips on the Mopan, Macal and other rivers by tube, raft and canoe.

8 Visit a butterfly farm
Belize now has six butterfly farms and centers (see page 70). Kids will enjoy

seeing one, though after that their interest may wane. For kids, we especially recommend Tropical Wings near San Ignacio.

 # 9 Splash in a pool
A swimming pool makes any day more fun for kids. Increasingly, as part of the upscaling of Belize tourism, Belize hotels offer swimming pools. (See our list of the best ones, page 55). The ones at SunBreeze and Chan Chich are especially great for kids.

 # 10 Make friends with a quash
It may not be 100% "EC" (Ecologically Correct) but a number of Belize lodges have once-wild animals as pets. Often, these are animals that have been injured, and the managers are nursing them back to health. In other cases, such as with iguanas, the lodge may be raising these in a controlled program. In any event, the opportunity to see monkeys, small cats, coatimundis, iguanas, parrots and other animals up close and personal is a treat for kids. Among the hotels with animals around are Lamanai Outpost, Jaguar Paw, Banana Bank, Pook's Hill and Hotel San Ignacio.

5 'Hidden' Costs for Travelers in Belize

When figuring your travel budget, don't forget these "extras."

 # 1 Sales Tax of 8%
This new tax applies to nearly every purchase, from clothespins to car rentals. But it's better than the 15% VAT, which was eliminated in April 1999 (though not that much better, because in practice it's applied almost like a VAT, to purchases at most levels of distribution.)

 # 2 Hotel Tax of 7%
Applies to rooms only, not meals or other purchases.

 # 3 Air Departure Tax of US$15
Must be paid in cash at the time of airport check-in. Tax is less for Belizeans.

 # 4 Hotel Service Charge of 5% to 15%
Some hotels add a service charge; others suggest you tip employees directly.

 # 5 Credit Card Surcharge of 3% to 5%
Shops and hotels may add a surcharge of 3 to 5% of the total if you're paying by credit card. This is less common than it used to be, but it still happens.

5 Friendliest Places in Belize

Belizeans, by and large, are warm, open, and welcoming to visitors. You can make friends easily anywhere in Belize.

1 Corozal Town
Generally safe town, overlooked by most tourists, with Mexican influence and very nice people.

2 Hopkins Village
Small and still unspoiled Garifuna area with warm, friendly folks.

3 San Ignacio Town
Relaxed community with a Maya and Mestizo heritage.

4 Punta Gorda Town
The "real Belize" at the country's southern tip.

5 Belize City
Belize City has a well-deserved reputation for crime and hassle, but it also has some of the hardest-working, friendliest people in Belize — too bad the rascals are what most visitors hear about.

5 Extreme Adventures in Belize

1 Crawl the Reef
Charter a boat and spend your days puttering around the barrier reef, snorkeling the incredible water and eating freshly caught fish. Spend your nights sleeping deeply under the stars. That's a reef crawl, something that — due to the dangers of navigating the reef without years of local experience — very few visitors get to experience.

2 Kayak the Sea
Kayaking gets you even closer to the Caribbean and the reef. You can do it alone (with careful planning), but you may be more comfortable going with one of the adventure tour outfitters.

3 Explore the Caves
Cayo, Stann Creek and Toledo districts boast some of the largest and most extensive cave systems in Central America. Some have undiscovered Maya relics. Many have not been explored in modern times. Don't try serious spelunking in Belize without an experienced guide.

4 Ride the Rivers
Belize's rivers range from slow tropical waters to fast-moving clear streams. The experience of rafting, tubing or canoeing the rivers can be restful, or it can be fast and furious. Hook up with an experienced guide or tour operator, grab

your hat and ride the rivers!

5 (tie) Climb the Mountains
The Maya Mountains may not be tall — the highest peaks are around 3,700 feet — but with their rugged jungle terrain and tropical heat, they're a challenge for even the fittest hiker. The Cockscomb Preserve is a great place to experience Belize's mountains.

5 (tie) Bike the Back Roads
Biking, including mountain biking, is just getting started in Belize. Because Belize is so lightly populated outside the cities and towns, and there are so few cars, Belize is ideal for adventuresome bike trips. The Mountain Pine Ridge is especially awesome.

5 Tips on Special Interests and Needs
Here's information for those with special interests or needs in travel.

Handicapped Travelers
Physically challenged travelers will find very few handicap-access facilities in Belize. Rarely do hotels have rooms or facilities for those with handicaps. In addition, sandy beaches, rough roads, old buses, small boats and jungle terrain may pose difficulties. That being said, most Belizeans are hospitable and helpful to everyone, and we know people with severe physical restrictions who have traveled successfully in Belize. Check with your hotel or lodge in advance to see what type of facilities are available.

Gay and Lesbian
Belize does not have a high-profile gay and lesbian scene. You won't find openly gay bars or clubs. Technically, homosexuality remains illegal in Belize (although no one has been prosecuted in recent times.) However, Belizeans generally are easy-going about sexual matters — Belize welcomed a gay cruise ship visit when it was turned away from the Cayman Islands — and gay and lesbian travelers experience few if any difficulties. San Pedro is probably the best bet for gays, but it's definitely not Key West. Belize's first hotel for gay men, located on North Ambergris, closed after only a short time.

Senior Citizens
So-called senior citizens are an increasingly important segment of the Belize tourism market. Several hotels, including Lamanai Outpost, long have worked with Elder Hostel on special-interest trips for older travelers.

Kids
Belize can be the perfect antidote to malls, fast-food restaurants and video

parlors, because it offers none of those things. Kids with an interest in water, wildlife and outdoor adventure will love Belize. For more information, see 10 Best Things to Do with Kids, page 46.

Backpackers

It's often said that Belize is expensive for Central America, cheap for the Caribbean. Backpackers can find safe, clean and comfortable accommodations in most areas of Belize for under US$20 a night. Caye Caulker, Placencia village and San Ignacio offer the biggest selection of budget digs. Camping is possible at private camp grounds near San Ignacio, Corozal and elsewhere, in a few national parks and preserves such as Cockscomb, on some offshore cayes, and on private land with advance permission.

5 Good Options for Camping

At present, Belize attracts few campers or RV owners. Reason? Lack of facilities, and, at least in the past, discouragement by Belize authorities, who felt camping would encourage backpackers who spend little or nothing. Still, for the hardy camper or RV owner, Belize offers a new frontier. In most situations, a hammock is a better option than a tent. Who wants a fer-de-lance as a bedfellow? To camp on private land, you'll need permission of the owner or caretaker. No public camping is available on Ambergris Caye, Belize's most popular tourist destination.

Private Camp Sites
A number of lodging choices in Belize also offer camping space, usually for around US$5 a night or less. Many of these are in Cayo district, including **The Trek Stop, Clarissa Falls, Caesar's Place, Casa Maya, Cosmos, Midas, Bol's, Blue Mountain Rider, Hilltop Camping, Monkey Bay Wildlife Sanctuary** and **Ian Anderson's.** Camping is also available at **Jungle Drift Lodge** in Bermudian Landing, at **Clive's** in Placencia, and elsewhere.

RV Camps
Travel trailers and recreational vehicles rarely make it as far south as Belize. Those that do will not find the kind of campgrounds common in the U.S. and even in Mexico. Two campgrounds are in Northern Belize: **Caribbean Village** in Corozal Town and **Lagoon Campground** north of town on the road to the Chetumal border crossing offer basic hook-ups for around US$10 to $15 a night. Some lodges in rural areas allow RV boondocking on their property.

National Parks
Camping generally is prohibited in Belize's national parks and preserves without advance permission from the Forestry Department in Belmopan. The exceptions are **Cockscomb Preserve** in Stann Creek District which has a small

campground (reserve through the Belize Audubon Society), and near Augustine village in the **Mountain Pine Ridge**. There also are camp sites near **Five Blues Lake National Park** at St. Margaret's village.

Safari Camps

This is an option for those who want to save money but prefer the safety and comfort of a raised platform and other amenities. The **Macal River Safari Camp** at Chaa Creek in Cayo has the most upscale version, at around US$50 per person, with nicely furnished tents set up on platforms, and hearty meals provided. The **Monkey Bay** private reserve (there's a river, a few monkeys nut no bay) near Belmopan offers, at US$5 a person, a more basic version.

Remote Cayes

Kayakers and other sea travelers can usually find a place to camp, in primitive splendor, on remote cayes. However, note that many cayes, including some nearest the coast, are fringed with mangroves and offer poor camping and zillions of mosquitoes. Most of Belize's islands are privately owned, so if there's anyone around, ask permission before hanging your hammock. Half Moon Caye, in the first marine reserve in Belize, offers great camping, though getting there costs a lot of money and time — ask at the park warden's office near the lighthouse for permission to camp.

5 Way-Off-the-Beaten Path 'Finds'

Most visitors to Belize end up on Ambergris Caye, in Cayo and Placencia. Those who spend more time in the country eventually visit lower profile destinations such as Corozal Town, Dangriga or Hopkins. But Belize also has small, out of the way spots which get almost no visitors. They're not for everybody, but they offer a refreshingly different experience. Here are five:

1 Sarteneja Peninsula

Less than two hours from Orange Walk Town, Sarteneja village, on the sea is a place where's there's not much to do and not much to see. That's its appeal. En route, you'll pass prosperous Mennonite farms, the beautiful Progresso Lagoon and sleepy villages where the main language is Spanish. Shipstern Nature Reserve, near Sarteneja village, is a bird-watcher's paradise.

2 Remote Cayes

We're not talking about "popular" spots like South Water Caye, which are great, but the really obscure cayes off the central and southern coasts of Belize. Some of these are just spits of sand, but, as with the barrier reef itself, these are the essence of the Caribbean that only a lucky few get to see. So, next trip, hire a boat (it won't be cheap) and get out to Goff's Caye or the Snake or Sapodilla Cayes.

3 Blue Creek, San Filipe and Rural Orange Walk District

Orange Walk Town is the second largest urban area in Belize, but its attractions for visitors are few and far between. Once out of the town, though, heading west, you're back in the real Belize, rolling farmland, small villages, and well-turned out Mennonite areas such as Blue Creek and Shipyard. From here, you can drive to Lamanai or Programme for Belize and Gallon Jug lands.

4 Monkey River Town

Still called a town, though it's now just a small village, Monkey River Town is where the Monkey River, teeming with birds and wildlife, meets the Caribbean. As more people visit here on tours from Placencia, and with improvements of the road to Monkey River from the Southern Highway, this area is getting more "tourism infrastructure" including several small hotels and restaurants.

5 Spanish Lookout

Next time, instead of heading into the Mountain Pine Ridge, turn off the Western Highway in the other direction and spend an afternoon in Spanish Lookout. This is a Mennonite area that may remind you more of Iowa than Belize.

5 Best Guided Tours in Belize

An attractive thing about travel in Belize is that, especially if you have a car, you can travel independently, go at your own pace, and not have to rely on expensive guided tours. But guided tours also have their advantages: You get the benefit of highly knowledgeable local guides (all guides in Belize must be licensed and pass fairly rigorous tests) and you can let someone else worry about the driving and the details of getting around. Here are our picks for the most interesting tours. Due to large number of guides and the fact that tours vary depending on where they originate, we are not able to make recommendations on specific guides or tour operators.

1 Tikal

Though Tikal is in Guatemala, not Belize, it heads our tour list because the ruins here are astounding. Tikal's setting in the jungle is incredible, the ruins are excavated so you get a sense of the scale and power of the site, and the trip (by road) through the Petén is interesting. Many visitors take a day van tour from one of the operators in San Ignacio, but tours also operate from Belize City and elsewhere, and there are daily flights from Belize City to Flores.

2 Half Moon Caye

Even if you're not a diver, a day boat trip from San Pedro to Lighthouse Reef, the Blue Hole and Half Moon Caye is an experience not to be overlooked. It can be a rough, long ride, but you'll see an extraordinary side of the Caribbean, with indescribably beautiful water, sea life and classic deserted islands.

3 (tie) Lamanai

The appeal of this tour is partly the trip there, by boat up the New River and New Lagoon. The ruins, though not large and not extensively excavated, are interesting, and you'll likely see a lot of birds and wildlife, including howler monkeys.

3 (tie) Caracol

Quite a few visitors choose to do Caracol independently, and (except in rainy weather) that can be a good option if you have a four-wheel drive vehicle. There's a visitor center at the site, and guides to show you around. However, if you're squeamish about long drives in remote jungle areas, a tour (usually from the San Ignacio area) may be preferable. The tour takes you through a variety of ecosystems, from piney woods to broadleaf jungle. Most include stops at waterfalls, the Rio Frio caves and elsewhere.

5 Monkey River

This trip, usually originating in Placencia, gets positive reactions from nearly everyone who takes it. A good guide will show you a lot of wildlife on the lagoon, along the river, and in the bush.

Best Golf and Tennis in Belize

"Very limited" is the only way to describe tennis and golf opportunities in Belize. In the years to come, we expect to see development of more golf courses and tennis courts, but right now these are your choices:

Golf: A new 9-hole course on Caye Chapel is the only place for visitors to play. It's a stunning setting, but development of this course was, to the say the least, controversial, with allegations of improper dredging around the reef. Environmentalists worry about the impact such a golf course will have on the reef and sea ecology.

Tennis: The newer facilities are the courts at Inn at Robert's Grove in Seine Bight (Placencia). Journey's End on North Ambergris also has courts.

Hotels with Air Conditioning

Only a few years ago, air conditioning was virtually unheard of in Belize (considering the price of electricity, no wonder). Now, as part of the upscaling trend in the tourism industry in Belize, many hotels have it. Here's a list — not all-inclusive by any means — of hotels with A/C. Note that on Ambergris Caye, nearly all hotels and condotels have air conditioning. In Belize City, most of the better hotels do. Elsewhere, air conditioning is still rare.

(Listed Alphabetically)
Alajuila Suites, Ambergris Caye
Banana Beach, Ambergris Caye
Barrier Reef Hotel (some units), Ambergris Caye
Belizean Reef Suites, Ambergris Caye
Belize Yacht Club, Ambergris Caye
Bellevue Hotel, Belize City
Biltmore Plaza, Belize City
Bull Frog Inn, Belmopan
Caribbean Villas, Ambergris Caye
Caribe Island Resort, Ambergris Caye
Casa Caribe, Ambergris Caye
Casa Solana, Ambergris Caye
Changes in Latitudes B&B, Ambergris Caye
Chateau Caribbean, Belize City
Coconuts, Ambergris Caye
Colton House (some units), Belize City
Coral Bay Villas, Ambergris Caye
Corona del Mar/Woody's, Ambergris Caye
Cottage Colony (some units), St. George's Caye
D-Victoria, Orange Walk Town
El Pescador (some units), Ambergris Caye
Embassy Hotel, Belize City
Essene Way, Ambergris Caye
Exotic Caye Resort/Playador, Ambergris Caye
Fiesta Inn, Belize City
Great House, Belize City
Hide-a-Way Sports Lodge (some units), Ambergris Caye
Holiday Hotel, Ambergris Caye
Hotel Del Rio (some units), Ambergris Caye
Inn at Robert's Grove, Seine Bight (Placencia)
Iguana Reef Inn, Caye Caulker
Jaguar Paw, Belmopan Area
Jaguar Reef, Sittee Point
Journey's End, Ambergris Caye
Lighthouse Reef Resort, Northern Two Caye
Lily's, Ambergris Caye
Mata Chica, Ambergris Caye
Mata Rocks, Ambergris Caye
Mayan Princess, Ambergris Caye
Nautical Inn, Seine Bight (Placencia)
The Palms, Ambergris Caye
Paradise Resort Hotel (some units), Ambergris Caye
Paradise Villas, Ambergris Caye
Pyramid Island Resort, Caye Chapel
Radisson Fort George, Belize City
Ramon's Village, San Ignacio
Rock's Inn, Ambergris Caye
Royal Orchid, Belize City
Royal Palms, Ambergris Caye
Ruby's (new units), Ambergris Caye
Rum Point Inn (new units), Placencia
San Ignacio Hotel (some units), San Ignacio
Seven Seas Hotel, Ambergris Caye
Spindrift Hotel, Ambergris Caye
SunBreeze, Ambergris Caye

Sunset Beach Resort, Ambergris Caye
The Tides (some units), Ambergris Caye
Tony's Inn, Corozal Town
Tropica, Ambergris Caye
Victoria House, Ambergris Caye
Villas at Banyan Bay, Ambergris Caye

10 Great Swimming Pools

You may not come to Belize to swim in a pool, but after a hot day on the sea or in the bush, it's great to splash in a clean, clear, cool pool. Here are some of the best pools:

1 Chan Chich Lodge, Gallon Jug, Orange Walk District
Like being in a pool in the jungle, without the bugs.

2 Inn at Robert's Grove, Seine Bight (Placencia)
With a view of the sea.

3 Ramon's, Ambergris Caye
This new pool replaces what was the oldest pool on the island.

4 SunBreeze, Ambergris Caye
Nice and shady.

5 Maruba Spa, Belize District
Exotic.

6 Captain Morgan's, Ambergris Caye
Big and enticing.

7 Jaguar Paw, Belmopan Area
Pop from your air-conditioned room for splash in the pool.

8 Jaguar Reef, Sittee Point
At last, a pool in the Hopkins area.

9 Radisson Fort George, Belize City
Not one but two.

10 Nautical Inn, Seine Bight (Placencia)
Joins the move to pools in Placencia.

10 New Hotels to Check Out

Here are new hotels in Belize, some so new even we haven't visited them yet.

Beaches and Dreams, Sittee Point
Three Canadian-owned cabins on the beach south of Jaguar Reef Lodge, getting rave reviews for food and accommodations.

Belize Odyssey, Caye Caulker
Another in the continued movement to bring air conditioning to dear Caye Corker.

Cayo Espanto
On a private island near Ambergris Caye, this ultra-deluxe (and very pricey) new spot reportedly is doing well.

Green Heaven Lodge, San Ignacio
Cabañas and pool 5 miles from San Ignacio.

Miller's Landing, Placencia
New small spot with pool.

Mopan River Resort, Benque Viejo del Carmen
Opening November 1999 as an "all-inclusive," with 12 cabañas on the Mopan River near Benque.

Placencia Lagoon Resort
Not on the Placencia peninsula but across the lagoon on Malacate Beach near Independence, with 8 thatch cabañas.

The Tides, Ambergris Caye
New spot north of San Pedro Town, operated by locals Patojo and Sabrina Paz, perfect for divers; a good value, and word-of-mouth is very strong.

Tipple Tree Beya Inn, Hopkins
Budget spot on the beach in Hopkins; this is just one of several new budget digs in up-and-coming Hopkins.

White Ridge Inn, Gales Point
Small spot near Gales Point, open December to April only; similarly named development in this lightly touristed area reportedly is in the planning stage.

10 Belizean Taste Treats

Belizean food isn't fancy. The best of it is honest and simple, made with care using local ingredients. Belize cooking increasingly reflects the country's cultural gumbo. With luck, you can enjoy Mexican-style escabeche and tortillas one day, Garifuna-style fish with coconut milk the next, and Creole cow foot soup the day after that.

1 Beans and Rice
The quintessential Belizean dish, beans and rice comes in as many varieties as there are Belizean cooks. You'll have it with red beans, black beans or pinto beans. It's seasoned with salt pork, salt beef or smoked turkey, often with coconut milk, garlic and onion, sometimes with bell pepper. Usually, beans and rice are served as a side dish to stew chicken or beef, or with fish. Any way you get it, it's tasty, filling and cheap.

2 Lobster
Belize's spiny lobster may not be as big as its Maine cousin, but it's delicious almost any way you can prepare it — broiled, boiled, grilled, baked, in fritters, soups, salads and bisques, and even fried or topping a pizza. But do your part to protect the lobster for future generations — don't eat it out of season (February 15 to June 15) even if you're told it's frozen.

3 Stew Chicken
Another Belize favorite, stew chicken gets part of its special flavor from red or black recado (achiote) seasoning.

4 Conch Fritters
Conch is delicious grilled, or stewed in lime juice in ceviche, but we like it best in fritters, fried in a light batter with an ice-cold Belikin. Conch is in season October to June.

5 Grilled Red Snapper
Catch it and cook it the same day. Eat it while you enjoy the breeze from the Caribbean. It doesn't get much better than that.

6 Fresh Fruit
Nothing starts a tropical day better than fresh fruit, and a variety of fruits is available in Belize for those not too lazy to walk out and pick some — many kinds of mangoes (in prime season in the spring), pineapples, papaya, bananas, watermelon, craboo and tamarind.

7 Boil Up
This Creole favorite, fish boiled with plantains, yams and potatoes, and served with a tomato sauce and a boiled bread, is not seen much in restaurants.

8 Serre and Hoodut
One of the best-known Garifuna dishes -- fish cooked in coconut milk with plantains.

9 Fried Chicken

Belizeans seem to love fried chicken more than Americans love hamburgers. A couple of pieces of chicken, potato salad, beans and rice and a red Fanta make a good meal anytime.

10 Fry Jacks

It's just fried bread dough, but with mango jam and a cup of Gallon Jug or Guatemalan coffee, it's mighty good.

5 Refreshing Belizean Drinks

1 Belikin Beer

Regular Belikin, brewed in vast quantities by Barry Bowen's Belize Brewing Co. Ltd., in the green bottle with the Altun Ha temple on the front, is cheaper and, many think, tastier than the Premium variety. Buy it by the case for U3$10.75 including tax

2 Belikin Stout

Not quite up to Guiness (which Bowen also brews, under license) but a hearty brew that builds the blood, whatever that means.

3 Parrot Rum

Gold Duurley's from Traveller's is smooth and gentle to both the body and the soul.

4 Caribbean Rum

Cullo'n gold rum is drinkable; we find the Caribbean White a little too rough and ready.

5 Red Fanta

Red Fanta could be the national drink of Belize. Orange Fanta also is widely appreciated.

5 Best Grocery Stores

In Belize City are several modern supermarkets, though they are not as large or as well stocked as many supermarkets in Mexico, the U.S. and Canada. Most grocery items in Belize are more expensive than in supermarkets back home, and selections are more limited.

1 Save-U Supermarket, San Cas Plaza, Belize City

Save-U advertises that it's the store with "glitter and glamour." We don't know about that, but it does have a good selection of grocery and household items, plenty of parking, air conditioning and even automatic doors.

 # 2 Brodies, 2 1/2 Miles Northern Highway, Belize City
James Brodie & Co. Ltd. has been in Belize for more than 100 years. This grocery, which opened in 1996, has clean, well-lit shopping with plenty of parking.

 # 3 Brodies, Albert and Regent Streets, Belize City
An institution for groceries and more in beautiful downtown Belize City. Besides this and the Northern Highway store, there also is a Brodies outpost in Belmopan.

 # 4 Celina's Superstore, 43 Burns Avenue, San Ignacio
Cayo's general store, with groceries plus dry goods, electronics and even insurance. Prices are a bit high, some say.

 # 5 (tie) Rock's II, Coconut Drive, Ambergris Caye
A bit smaller than the original Rock's in San Pedro Town, about the size of a U.S. convenience store

 # 5 (tie) San Pedro Supermarket, San Pedro Town, Ambergris Caye
About the size of the two Rocks stores, this grocerette is handy for those in the north end of town and on North Ambergris.

Honorable Mention: **Ro-Mac's Supermarket,** 27 Albert Street, Belize City. Recently purchased by Santiago Castillo.

5 Best Markets

Belize's markets are not as colorful as those in Guatemala or Mexico, but here you'll usually find tasty local fruits and vegetables, in season. Saturday is usually market day, although vendors at some markets may be set up all week.

 # 1 San Ignacio Market, Cayo
Fresh fruit and vegetables from Cayo farms make the Saturday market here the best in the country. If you're going across the Guatemala border, Melchor has a small daily market with good deals on edibles and crafts.

 # 2 "Temporary" Market, north side of Haulover Creek, Belize City
This where the vendors from the old colonial market were "temporarily" moved in 1993.

 # 3 Belize City Commercial Center, Belize City
The new city market, with its marble floors, is luxe, but it lacks the energy and atmosphere of the old city market. Changes are said to be ahead for this venue.

 # 4 Punta Gorda Market
Colorful mix of Toledo folks, plus inexpensive fruits and vegetables.

 # 5 Corozal Market
On the breezy bay front in Corozal Town.

10 Best Souvenirs of Belize

Belize does not have the rich crafts tradition of its neighbors Guatemala and
Belize, and gift shops offer the usual collection of off-color T-shirts and bad-
taste geegaws, but there are handcrafts, furniture, music cassettes, local foods
and drinks and other items that make good souvenirs or gifts from Belize.
Don't buy items that contribute to the destruction of endangered wildlife or the
reef, such as items made from coral, including "black coral" and turtle or
tortoise shells. The export of Maya artifacts is strictly prohibited. Some gift
shops in Belize also carry high-quality textiles and other items from
Guatemala. The following items worth buying are listed in no particular order.

• **Local music tapes.** Ain't we got rhythm? Belize music goes in every
direction, from Creole brukdown and cunga to Garifuna punta rock and
Mestizo marimba, not to mention Caribbean-style ska, reggae and calypso, or,
of course, imported rap. Classic Belize artists include the world-famous punta
masters Andy Palacio, Barranco-born, and the Original Turtle Shell Band,
Creole kings Mr. Peter's Boom and Chime and Bredda David, but young
hipsters will quickly smell out the best new talents. Cubola Production's
Stonetree Records is a top Belize record studio. Avoid buying pirated tapes.

• **Wood crafts.** Belize has a number of talented carvers who turn out well-
made kitchen bowls and sea and wildlife art from zericote and other local
woods. One of the best places to buy authentic Belizean crafts at fair prices is
the **National Handicraft Center** on Fort Street in Belize City.

• **Contemporary Belizean art.** Established artists such as Walter Castillo,
originally from Nicaragua, who now has a shop, Belizean Arts, in San Pedro,
and Benjamin Nicholas, a Garifuna with a studio in Dangriga, command high
prices for original work, but Belize also has a growing number of young,
highly creative artists working in various media. The **Image Factory,** a
gallery at 91 N. Front Street in Belize City, is a good place to see their work
and, sometimes, to meet the artists themselves.

• **Maya slate carvings.** Common in Guatemala, flat slate carvings with
traditional Maya themes are also available in Belize, by the Garcia sisters and
others.

• **Local hot sauces and jams.** Several Belizean companies produce delicious jams and addictive hot sauces. Two of the best are Marie Sharp's — sometimes available in the U.S. but the selection is wider in Belize — and Barry Bowen's Gallon Jug Estate lines. The cheapest place to buy these are at the large Belize City supermarkets, but gift shops and hotels also carry them.

• **Belize-grown coffee.** Most of Belize is at altitudes too low for high-quality coffee, but Barry Bowen's farm at Gallon Jug, at only 400 feet elevation, is getting into coffee production in a sizable way. The result is a tasty and unusual product of Belize. Gallon Jug has about 170,000 coffee plants ranging in age from six months to 10 years. The coffee is grown, processed, roasted and packed on the Bowen farm. The 1998 crop (cherries are picked from September to February) yielded about 25,000 pounds of roasted coffee. Gallon Jug Estates coffee, whole bean or ground, is widely sold in Belize. Hidden Valley Inn also produces a little coffee, available at the hotel.

• **Wood furniture.** Clam shell chairs and other furniture from teak, mahogony and other tropical woods made by Mennonite and other Belizean furniture makers offer high-quality and high-value souvenirs at remarkably reasonable prices. Some shops will pack and ship these items for you.

• **Belize postage stamps.** Belize postage stamps make colorful, inexpensive and easy-to-carry souvenirs, although the stamps themselves are not printed in Belize.

• **Natural remedies of Belize.** Belize's bush doctors and natural healers have developed a wide variety of herbal and natural medicines, and many a traveler has found that some of these seem to really work, especially on bug bites and upset tummies. Dr. Rosita Arvigo's Rainforest Remedies line is widely sold in Belize, but other salves, tinctures and ointments are available for nearly every ailment.

• **Belize brews.** Local rums — the darker ones are smoother — from Cuello's or Traveller's distilleries bring back the flavor of Belize after you get home. Belikin beer is also a popular souvenir. And, no, Belikin is not distributed outside of Belize.

Natural Wonders

Photo by Fran Dwight

Pantera onca, *AKA tiger or jaguar, eyes a visitor at the Belize Zoo*

5 Wonderful National Parks and Reserves

Belize is making a terrific effort to preserve its natural land and sea resources for future generations. Here are national parks and reserves which won't disappoint you:

1 Cockscomb Basin Wildlife Preserve, Stann Creek District
The world's first jaguar preserve, this lush jungle reserve of more than 100,000 acres is a must-see for anyone interested in natural Belize. New trails are open to Victoria Peak, one of the highest points in Belize.

2 Half Moon Caye Natural Monument, Lighthouse Reef
Belize's first nature preserve, Half Moon Caye is a beautiful island on Lighthouse Reef, with 10,000 acres of surrounding reef.

3 Mountain Pine Ridge Reserve, Cayo District
More than 300 square miles of nearly unpopulated land in Western Belize. Controlled logging is allowed.

4 Rio Bravo Conservation and Management Area, Orange Walk District
More than 150,000 acres of jungle, including mahogany forest, in Orange Walk District, privately managed by Programme for Belize.

5 (tie) Crooked Tree Wildlife Sanctuary, Crooked Tree
This is bird city in Belize. The sanctuary boundaries encompass several large lagoons, including Crooked Tree and Revenge.

5 (tie) Community Baboon Sanctuary, Bermudian Landing
More than 1,000 black howler monkeys are now safe in the eight villages making up the sanctuary.

Other recommended parks and preserves:
- Bacalar Chico National Park and Marine Reserve, Ambergris Caye
- Blue Hole National Park, Hummingbird Highway
- Five Blues Lakes National Park, Hummingbird Highway
- Hol Chan, Ambergris Caye
- Tapir Mountain Nature Reserve, Belmopan Area
- Laughing Bird Caye National Park, off Placencia
- Guanacaste National Park, Belmopan

10 Delightful Denizens of the Wild

1 Jaguar *Panthera onca*
Often called tiger by Belizeans, the jaguar is the largest cat in the Western Hemisphere. The spotted jaguar and the black jaguar are the same species.

There may be more than 1,000 jaguars in Belize, but you need extraordinary luck to see one of these beautiful nocturnal animals, except at the Belize Zoo, which has both spotted and black jaguars. There are usually a couple of dozen jaguar sightings each year at Chan Chich Lodge in Orange Walk District. Belize has four other species of wild cats: puma, margay, jaguarundi and ocelot.

2 Mountain Cow *Tapirus bairdii*
Baird's tapir, locally called mountain cow, the national animal of Belize, eats only veggies and is shy and nonaggressive.

3 Black Howler Monkey *Alouatta pigra*
Howlers, sometimes called baboons in Belize, are rare, found only in parts of Belize, Guatemala, and Mexico. Almost wiped out by disease in the 1950s, they are making a comeback in Belize, thanks to efforts at protection, such as at Community Baboon Sanctuary, and through reintroduction in Cayo and Stann Creek districts and elsewhere.

4 Blue Morpho Butterfly *Morpho peleides*
Belize has nearly 700 species of butterflies, but the Blue Morpho, with its electric blue color, is perhaps the most striking.

5 Quash (White-nose coatimundi) *Nasua narica*
Coatimundis, relatives of the raccoon, are cute as the devil. They're smart and have a keen sense of smell. Sometimes kept as pets in Belize.

6 Margay Cat *Leopardus wiedii*
Loves to climb trees, looks like an overgrown house cat, with lots of kittenish charm.

7 Green Iguana *Iguana iguana*
Several species of iguanas make their home in Belize. An effort is underway to promote the raising of green iguanas, locally prized as a chicken-like dish.

8 Red-eyed Tree Frog *Agalychnis callidras*
Bulging ruby-red eyes and a green body — what a concept! Found in lowland wet forest areas.

9 Kinkajou *Potos flavus*
Looks a little like a monkey, but like the coati it's a relative of the raccoon.

10 Bush dog (Tayra) *Eira barbara*
Weasel-like animal often visits Belize gardens in southern and western Belize.

10 Spectacular Birds

Belize has more than 600 species of birds. For serious birders, the sighting of an obscure finch brings joy to one's life list; most of the rest of us are easily impressed by big colorful splashy birds like these:

 # 1 Keel-billed Toucan *Ramphastos sulfuratus*
"Banana Bill" is the national bird of Belize. It frequents lowland forests under 2,000 feet and is found in many parts of Belize, including, commonly, on tee-shirts in San Pedro.

 # 2 Jabiru Stork *Jabiru mycteria*
This white-bodied stork, 4 to 5 feet tall with a wing span of 8 feet or more, gives Big Bird a run for his money in the size department. The Jabiru is the largest wild bird in the Americas. It loves marshes and lagoons — Crooked Tree Lagoon (aka Northern Lagoon) and Mexico Lagoons are good places to see one, especially December to March.

 # 3 Scarlet Macaw *Ara macao*
With its wings of scarlet, yellow and blue and its brilliant scarlet head, breast and tail, this bird is unmistakable. Flocks can be seen in the Cockscomb Preserve and near Red Bank village.

 # 4 Red-footed Booby *Sula sula*
Several thousand endangered Red-footed Boobies make their home on Half Moon Caye. Another type of red-footed booby makes it home in timeshares on Ambergris Caye.

 # 5 Oscellated Turkey *Agriocharis ocellata*
More like a peacock than like its cousin, the barnyard turkey, the Oscellated can be seen on the ground in several parts of Belize, including commonly around Gallon Jug and at Caracol.

 # 6 Great Curassow *Crax rubra*
This turkey-sized bird with a wacky hair-do inhabits humid forest areas. Quam is its local name.

 # 7 King Vulture *Sarcoramphus papa*
This warty old fellow with naked head may remind you of one of your uncles. Fairly common in the Cockscomb Preserve but declining in some other areas of Belize due to loss of habitat.

 # 8 Magnificent Frigate Bird *Fregata magnificens*
Common on Ambergris Caye and other cayes, and even around Belize City,

frigate birds swoop through the sky, like street hoods in the port city, stealing food from their neighbors.

 # 9 Slaty-tailed Trogan   *Trogan massena*
Belize does not have the Resplendent Quetzal — to see the avion Liberace you'll have to go to Guatemala — but this colorful trogan, or ramatutu, is in the same family, as are the Collared, Violaceous and Black-headed trogans.

 # 10 Yellow-headed Parrot *Amazona ochrocephala*
Belize has eight species of parrots and parakeets — parakeets have pointed tails, parrots have square tails. Yellow-headed parrots, unfortunately often trapped and caged, can be seen in rural areas of Belize, including in Cayo and northern Belize.

10 Wild Things to Watch Out For

Belize is rich in life forms, including some that are not very nice to human beings. Fortunately, most visitors to Belize aren't bothered by these denizens of the wild, save for the occasional mozzie or no-see-um bites.

 # 1 No-see-ums (sand flies, sand fleas, midge gnats, *purrujas*)
These buggers are twice as mean as mozzies — watch out for them near mangrove swamps and on a windless day on the coast or cayes; Avon Skin-So-Soft or bug juice with DEET may help.

 # 2 Mozzies
Some mosquitoes in Belize do carry dangerous diseases including malaria and dengue fever. Many visitors to Belize are surprised, though, that mosquitoes are not as bad as they feared. The nearly constant winds on the cayes keep mozzies at bay, and much of Cayo District escapes the plague of these bugs. They are worse in the late summer after periods of rain, and in southern Belize, which gets more rain than any other part of the country.

 # 3 Botfly
This little horror, happily not a problem for most visitors, gets the help of a mosquito to place its egg under your skin. The larva then grows to the size of your thumb— yecch! Lure the bugger out with a slab of fatback or bacon placed over the entrance; kill it by smothering it to death with vaseline or glue; or apply the sap of the bot killer tree, or some say, a piece of tobacco.

 # 4 Yellow-jawed Tommygoff (fer-de-lance)
This highly poisonous snake attacks aggressively. It has heat-seeking fangs and can strike accurately even in the dark. Avoid it, and if by rare chance you are bitten get medical attention immediately. Belize has about 20 types of

poisonous snakes of which "only" nine are deadly.

5 Scorpions
These are common all over Belize. They are often present in the walls of buildings (avoid leaving wet towels out) or in thatch roofs. For most species in Belize, the sting hurts, but not too much worse than the sting of a wasp, and isn't fatal.

6 Killer Bees
The stings of Africanized bees hurt no more than those of ordinary honeybees, but killer bees are far more aggressive and ill-tempered. They have killed many cattle and other livestock in Belize, and in Costa Rica more than a score of human deaths have been attributed to killer bee attacks. Virtually all the honeybees you see in Belize are now Africanized. They are present in most areas, even on Ambergris Caye. If you stumble on a hive, try to get under a roof (bees usually won't follow you under a shelter) or into water.

7 "Alligators"
Called thus by many Belizeans, but Belize actually has only crocodiles, the larger American and the smaller Morelet's. They are present in both fresh-water lagoons and in salt water, in mangrove areas of the coast and cayes. Attacks on humans are rare.

8 Warries (White-Lipped Peccary)
Peccaries are related to pigs. White-Lipped Peccaries, now rare in Belize, travel in large herds. If you hear loud bellowing, screeching and tooth-clacking (and don't happen to be in Big Daddy's late at night), climb the nearest tree, as warries can be hazardous to your health.

9 Tarantulas
You may see one of these furry balls of fun on the rain forest floor or even on Ambergris Caye. Their bite can be painful but isn't serious. Some people keep them as pets.

10 Vampire Bats
Belize does have vampire bats, whose bite may cause rabies, but unless you sleep outside a lot without clothes on, don't worry. Belize's many species of bats do worlds of good, from eating mozzies to pollinating fruit. Belizeans call this and several other species of bats "rat bats."

5 Cool Trees

More than 4,000 flowering plants and 700 species of trees are native to Belize. Here are some of the coolest:

 # 1 Cohune Palm *Orbignya cohune*
The cohune palm — locally pronounced Ko-HOON — grows over much of mainland Belize. It's a beautiful and highly useful tree. Its fronds are used as a cheap roof thatch, its fruit provide oil and its husks can be burned for fuel. Considered a symbol of fertility by the ancient Maya, today it is often a flag for hidden Maya ruins.

 # 2 Red Mangrove *Rhizophora mangle*
Mangroves — the dominant red, plus black and white mangroves — cover most of the coast and many of the cayes of Belize. Greedy developers would love to get rid of them so that their lots have a better view of the water, but mangroves are invaluable as protection against erosion, hurricane damage and as a nursery for sea life.

 # 3 Honduran Mahogany *Swietenia macrophylla*
The big-leafed mahogany is the national tree of Belize and appears on the country's flag. Logging has eliminated much of Belize's natural supply of these beautiful trees. You can see some in the Programme for Belize lands in Orange Walk District.

 # 4 Coconut Palm *Cocos nucifera*
Though not native to Belize, the coco palm, tall and stately, is the defining tree on many cayes. It is now being threatened by a disease called Lethal Yellowing, although injections of antibiotics can save individual trees.

 # 5 Ceiba *Ceiba pentandra*
The Ceiba — also known as the kapok or cotton tree — is one of the tallest and loveliest of all the trees in the jungle. You can spot it by its gray trunk and towering stature.

5 Most Scenic Drives

Belize does not have the drop-dead breathless scenery of highlands Guatemala or Costa Rica, but Belize's small population, uncut forests, and diverse ecosystems provide a uniquely Belizean brand of beauty. *Emory King's Driver's Guide to Beautiful Belize* and the ITMB *Belize Traveller's Map* will keep you from getting lost.

 # 1 Hummingbird Highway
Hands down, this road from Belmopan to near Dangriga is the most beautiful drive in Belize, and beyond the first miles near Belmopan, it is also the best road in Belize. (Resurfacing of the remaining miles should be completed in 1999.) The beginnings of the Maya Mountains, green and lush, are interrupted by the occasional citrus farm. You can't see them, but these limestone hills are

laced with vast networks of caves.

2 Road to Caracol
The road to Caracol begins with the bone-jarring routes from Georgeville or San Ignacio into the North Georgia-like scenery of the Mountain Pine Ridge. But once beyond Augustine/Douglas DeSilva, the real beauty begins. It is a vast and unpopulated area, close to Guatemala, and the road, though improved, is still no superhighway. When the butterflies are flying and the sky is blue, this is a magical, if rough, trip to the ruins of Caracol.

3 Road to Sarteneja and Progresso Lagoon
This little-traveled area of northern Belize provides glimpses of beauty to make up for the unpaved roadway. En route from Orange Walk Town, you'll enjoy seeing the Progresso Lagoon, prosperous Mennonite farms, and the isolated villages of Chunox and Sarteneja, on the Bay of Chetumal. On your return, if past the Progresso Lagoon you turn right instead of going back to Orange Walk, you can visit the village of Copper Bank and the ruins of Cerros.

4 Road to Chan Chich
Most people fly to Gallon Jug, but driving is a better way to see some of the real Belize (advance permission is needed to travel the privately owned sections of this route). This part of Orange Walk District is a country of Mennonite and other farms, small rural villages, and wild bush. As you drive through Programme for Belize and Gallon Jug lands, you'll likely see Oscellated turkeys and other rare wildlife. This is also one of the region's last remaining mahogany forests. The road to Lamanai, which turns off at San Felipe Village, is also a great drive.

5 (tie) Road to Gales Point and Southern Lagoon
The new coastal highway, or "shortcut" from Democracia to Stann Creek, is mostly an awful road, dusty in the dry season and muddy or flooded after rains. But the short section of unpaved road, from around Melinda about 10 miles north of Dangriga, to Gales Point, ending at the Colonial-style Manatee Lodge, is loaded with simple charm and unexpected beauty. The charm comes from the small Creole village of Gales Point, and the beauty of the Southern Lagoon, home to crocodiles, jabiru storks, and manatee.

5 (tie) Roads to Maya Villages near PG
While not an area of tremendous scenic beauty, the roads off the Southern Highway to the Maya villages near San Antonio and beyond are an education in history and culture. In rainy weather, the roads can become impassable even for four-wheel drives. Timbering activity is going on in this area. As paving is completed on more of the Southern Highway, and if — as has been proposed — the Southern Highway is completed into Guatemala, this area will be much

more visited than it is today. Come soon!

5 Best Butterfly Farms

Belize has nearly 700 species of butterflies. Some of the most beautiful and interesting of these can be seen up close and personal at one of Belize's six butterfly farms. Two of these, Green Hills and Fallen Stones, are seriously involved in the business of exporting pupae. The other butterfly places are, to one degree or another, set up as educational and informational facilities. For the casual visitor these educational facilities may even be of more interest.

1 Green Hills Butterfly Farm, Cayo District
Jan Meerman and Tineke Boomsma are serious about butterflies. (Meerman is writing a guidebook to the butterflies of Belize.) The setting, at Mile 8 of Mountain Pine Ridge Road, is beautiful.

2 Fallen Stones Butterfly Ranch, Toledo District
Ray Harberd and his staff (Mayas from San Pedro Columbia village) currently export about 20,000 pupae a year. There are about 35 species on display. The view into Guatemala from the Fallen Stones lodge is fabulous.

3 Blue Morpho Butterfly, Chaa Creek, Cayo
Part of the Natural History center at Chaa Creek Cottages, the butterfly farm focuses on the electric blue and incredibly beautiful *Morpho peleides*. Tours here are excellent.

4 Tropical Wings Butterfly Center, Cayo District
Butterflies are just one part of the Tropical Wings nature center, which has a variety of displays demonstrating the interrelationships of animals and plants in the tropical ecosystem. About 20 or 25 species are on display. Associated with The Trek Stop.

5 (tie) Xochil Ku, Indian Village, Orange Walk District
A small community-run center near the Lamanai Maya site.

5 (tie) Shipstern, Corozal District
Formerly a serious butterfly operation run by Jan Meerman, now of Green Hills, the butterfly center here, under the auspices of the Belize Audubon Society, now functions primarily for visitor education.

Reef and Sea

Boats docked at San Pedro, ready to head out for fishing, diving and other pleasures of the reef and sea

5 Beautiful Beaches

Belize isn't known for its world-class beaches. Mostly, that is due to the barrier reef, which reduces the wave action that over time builds wide, sandy beaches. Many caye and coastal beaches also have a lot of seagrass. However, most travelers to Belize agree that there are plenty of picture-perfect stretches of sand with swaying palms, just right for hanging a hammock. Here are a few:

1 Half Moon Caye and Lighthouse Reef Atoll
Belize's first marine preserve includes one of only four true atolls in the Western Hemisphere (three are in Belize, one is near Trinidad). Getting here takes time — two to three hours from San Pedro — but this is truly a stunning part of the Caribbean, with a half-moon shaped beach (hence the name).

2 Long and Middle Cayes and Glover's Reef Atoll
White sand, ridiculously clear and blue water, even whale sharks at some times of the year.

3 North Ambergris Caye
The north end of Ambergris has long stretches of beach, in some areas narrow and in others wide and sandy. Swimming and snorkeling from the shore are not that great, and more and more houses are being built in parts of this area, but overall the setting is idyllic.

4 Placencia Peninsula
The narrow strip of toast-colored sand runs some 16 miles along the peninsula.

5 (tie) Hopkins/Sittee Point
Similar to Placencia's beach, though not as long.

5 (tie) South Water Caye
Arguably one of the nicest getaways in Belize, with good snorkeling on the south end of the island not far from shore.

Honorable Mention: Ranguana Caye, Blackbird Caye, Sapodilla Cayes

5 Top Dives

1 Lighthouse Reef Atoll
The atoll farthest from the mainland offers diving with superb visibility and spectacular wall dives. The Blue Hole is worth doing ... once.

2 Glover's Reef Atoll
Glover's Reef is a biologically rich and diverse area, with lots of fish, sharks and sea life.

3 Turneffe Islands
This 30-mile long series of mangrove cayes and tiny islets, the third of Belize's atoll areas, offers diving in shallow reef rather than the steep wall diving of Glover's and Lighthouse.

4 Southern Reef
As you go south in Belize, the barrier reef lays farther offshore and is more pristine than to the north. Southern cayes are rich in bird and sea life.

5 Sapodilla Cayes, Far Southern Belize
Some of these remote cayes have been but lightly explored in modern times. Coral walls and broken reefs offer excellent diving.

10 Professional Dive Shops

Here are 10 dive shops, listed alphabetically, about which we get generally positive reports. This is not an all-inclusive list, and other dive shops may also do a good job. Often, small lesser-known dive shops provide more personal attention.

(Listed Alphabetically)
Amigos del Mar, San Pedro
Blue Hole Dive Center, San Pedro
Frenchie's, Caye Caulker
Gaz Cooper's, San Pedro
Hustlers, San Pedro
Patojo's, San Pedro
Placencia Dive Shop, Placencia
Ramon's Village, San Pedro
Rum Point Divers, Placencia
Sea Horse Divers, Placencia

5 Accessible Places for Great Snorkeling

There are literally thousands of spots in Belize's Caribbean where you can don a mask and jump into an enchanted undersea world. The catch is that most of these places are on or near the barrier reef or around remote islands. A boat charter or even a day trip will take you to some of the best snorkeling in the world. The snorkeling choices here are those that are accessible from the shore or via a short boat ride.

1 Hol Chan Marine Reserve, near Ambergris Caye
Hol Chan offers snorkelers lots of sea life and some beautiful coral. Careful -- currents here can be strong.

 # 2 Laughing Bird Caye, off Placencia
This small caye and marine park near Placencia makes a great snorkeling trip.

 # 3 Shark-Ray Alley, near Ambergris Caye
The draw here is the chance to swim with sharks (nurse sharks which generally aren't any danger to humans) and rays. Not as scary as you'd think.

 # 4 South Water Caye, off Dangriga
Snorkeling from shore on the south end of the island.

 # 5 French Louis Caye, off Placencia
Small mangrove fringed caye about six miles offshore, with excellent snorkeling.

10 Incredible Sea Creatures of Belize

 # 1 West Indian Manatee *Trichechus manatus*
The manatee, a distant relative of the elephant, is a gentle herbivore. It is an endangered species. There have been reports of the slaughter of families of manatees in Toledo District by Guatemalan fishermen. Manatees can be seen in the Southern Lagoon and along the coast and lagoons near Placencia, Hopkins, Punta Gorda, and elsewhere.

 # 2 Hammerhead Shark *Sphyrna zygaena*
This baby will get your attention. Real quick. Hammerheads can be seen around Glover and other atolls, and they occasionally come to town to see what's happening around Caulker or San Pedro.

 # 3 Whale Shark *Rhincodon typus*
Thought to be the biggest fish in the world, this gentle giant can be seen in Belize waters in April and May.

 # 4 Nurse Shark *Ginglymostoma cirratum*
If you want to amaze your friends with tales and photos of swimming with the sharks, cavorting with placid nurse sharks at Shark-Ray Alley near San Pedro, or elsewhere, is the way to do it.

 # 5 Loggerhead Turtle *Staurotypus triporcatus*
Three species of sea turtles — besides the loggerhead, the green and the hawksbill — nest in Belize, usually in the months of June through August.

 # 6 Bottlenose Dolphin *Tursiops truncatus*
These dolphins, smart, social and aware of humans, are common around the cayes and off the coast of Belize.

 # 7 Manta Ray *Manta hamiltoni*
These huge, mean-looking fellers are harmless to humans (though hell on plankton).

 # 8 Spiny Lobster *Panulirus* sp.
Ummmm, good. But only in season — mid-June to mid-February.

 # 9 Elkhorn Coral *Acropora palmata*
Just one of the fabulous corals on the living reef.

 # 10 Queen Angelfish *Holacanthus ciliaris*
This skittering blurb of color is one of many beautiful tropical fish in Belize waters.

10 Remote and Relaxing Island Getaways

Some of Belize's most appealing resorts are on remote islands and atolls. Most are oriented to divers or anglers. You'll have to make your own entertainment.

 # 1 Lighthouse Reef Resort, Northern Two Caye
Glorious isolation on 1,200 acres; great diving and fishing around the atolls; good beaches; even A/C — several types of accommodations.

 # 2 Pelican Beach Resort Cottages, South Water Caye
The Heron Cottage is what many believe Belize should always be. SWC offers fine snorkeling just off the beach at the south end of the island.

 # 3 Turneffe Island Lodge, Little Caye Bokel
Upgraded fish-camp style lodge; reasonable rates.

 # 4 (tie) Blackbird Caye, Turneffe Islands
Ten thatch cabañas.

 # 4 (tie) Manta Resort, Glover's Reef
Cabins and a larger house; affordable rates.

 # 6 (tie) Cottage Colony, St. George's Caye
Colonial cottages on a historical island; very reasonable rates.

 # 6 (tie) Little Water Resort, Little Water Caye
German-owned lodge on small private caye, with fine snorkeling and relaxin'.

 # 8 (tie) Ranguana Reef Resort, Ranguana Caye
Not fancy, but those who've tried the cabins here love the place.

 # 8 (tie) Blue Marlin Lodge, South Water Caye
Pleasant fish/dive lodge with cabañas.

 # 8 (tie) St. George's Lodge, St. George's Caye
Dive resort with good food about 8 miles off Belize City.

 # 10 (tie) French Louis Caye
Small mangrove-lined caye with excellent snorkeling; arrange a visit through Kitty's in Placencia.

 # 10 Glover's Atoll Resort
Basic cabins on Northeast Caye; beautiful setting, excellent value.

10 Good Places to Stay on Caye Caulker

While trying to move upmarket, Caye Caulker remains mostly a budget island, with a bit of funk and a few — but a few too many — pushy Rastaphonians and other off-islanders. Hotels here are mostly clean and neat, but far from fancy. Rates range from as little as US$10 to US$90 or so.

(Listed Alphabetically)
Anchorage
New hotel on the site of the original hotel of the same name, one of the first hotels on the island. Nice rooms with private baths and balconies.

Chocolate's
A one-room hotel, and a nice room it is.

Iguana Reef
Presently the most "upscale" place on the island, and also, at up to US$90 a night double in-season, the most expensive.

Seabeezzz
Friendly, family-run spot.

Seaview
Now run by Fred Prost, who formerly owned Parrot's Nest in Cayo.

Shirley's Guest House
Neat and trim, well run, near the airstrip.

1788 Motel
Newer spot near the Split, with comfortable rooms.

Tom's Hotel
Long popular with the budget crowd, Tom's has expanded and now has a wider choice of rooms.

Tree Tops Hotel
A real bargain, with very clean, comfortable rooms.

Tropical Paradise
A long-time favorite, with a good restaurant.

Also recommended: **Jimínez Cabañas, Barbara's Guest House, Monique's, Morgan's, Martinez Caribbean Inn**

5 Top Fishing Lodges

Belize has some of the best fishing in the world, for bonefish, tarpon, permit, snook and more. Here are five lodges that are known for good fishing and comfortable surroundings. Guides say October is the best month for big tarpon; December through February are the best months for snook; April and May are best for permit; bonefish bite all year, although cold fronts that come through occasionally in the winter, drive them from the flats to deeper water.

(Listed alphabetically)
Belize River Lodge, near Belize City
Offers a crewed and captained liveaboard fishing boat, a '58 Hatteras.

El Pescador, Ambergris Caye
Homey colonial atmosphere on North Ambergris.

Lillpat Sittee River Lodge
This upmarket fishing lodge is on the Sittee River near Hopkins.

Placencia Hotels
We can't single out one particular Placencia hotel as a top fishing lodge, but most hotels here offer access to fishing and to Placencia's excellent selection of fishing guides, including the Westby clan, Kevin Modera and Charles Cabral, and others.

Turneffe Flats Lodge
Beach-front cabins just a few hundred yards from the reef attract a clientele serious about fly fishing.

5 Boat Charters

Belize is not — and never will be — as big a chartering center as, for instance, the British Virgin Islands. For one thing, stiff winds, strong currents, choppy waters and the barrier reef with its hidden coral heads can make navigation dicey, even for sailors who know local waters.

(Listed alphabetically)
Belize River Lodge, near Belize City
Offers a crewed and captained liveaboard fishing boat, a '58 Hatteras.

Crewed Charters, St. Thomas, USVI
This Virgin Islands based outfit offers limited chartering in Belize.

Peter Singfield Charters, Xaibe Village, Corozal District
Probably the best value in the Caribbean. US$400 per person, all inclusive, for seven days on a Belizean sailing sloop.

Tortola Marine Management, Ambergris Caye
This outpost of BVI-based TMM has a small fleet of catamarans (sail and motorized) for bareboat and skippered chartering. Rates vary depending on the boat and time of year, but range from around US$2,200 to more than US$6,000 a week, not including provisions. Skippers are an additional US$100 per day.

Windsong Charters, Punta Gorda
Based at Orange Point Marina in PG, Windsong offers MacGregor 26s, either bareboat or captained. Bareboat rate for a charter running from Sunday to Saturday is US$1,850. Provisioning is available from around US$228.

Honorable Mention: *Winnie Estelle,* San Pedro

Best Liveaboards

For serious divers, liveaboards are a great way to get maximum dive time at the best dive sites in Belize, including Lighthouse and Turneffe atolls.

 # 1 (tie) *Belize Aggressor III,* **Aggressor Fleet**
Up to 18 divers enjoy first-rate accommodations and food.

 # 1 (tie) *Belize Wave Dancer,* **Peter Hughes Diving**
120-foot boat accommodates up to 20 divers in comfort.

Honorable Mention: *Offshore Express,* San Pedro

Ambergris Caye

A statue of St. Joseph at the Catholic church on Front Street (Barrier Reef Drive) in San Pedro

10 Top Ambergris Hotels

Note that Ambergris Caye condotels and budget hotels are listed separately.

1 Caribbean Villas

Not the most luxurious hotel, no beach to speak of, no pool, but friendly management by Wil and Susan Lala and staff makes all the difference in this comfortable apartment-style resort south of San Pedro Town.

2 (tie) Cayo Espanto

Small, upscale development on private island a few minutes west of Ambergris.

2 (tie) Mata Chica

Trendy, beautifully designed new spot far up on North Ambergris. One of Ambergris' most romantic restaurants. No pool. Nice beach. Not for everybody.

4 Sunbreeze

A recent makeover including pool has turned this Holiday Inn-style motel into one of the better, and best-located, choices on the island. Big rooms, with all the modcons. Italian restaurant and Gaz Cooper's dive shop on site.

5 Victoria House

Lovely beach-front setting about two miles south of town; potential, not always realized, of being one of the best resorts in Belize; variety of accommodations, some very pricey.

6 Ramon's

Extremely popular spot, especially for first timers to Belize. With 60 units, more crowded than we'd like, but still retains its thatch-and-sand ambiance. Beautiful new pool. Best beach in or near San Pedro Town. Rates are surprisingly high.

7 (tie) Coconuts

Friendly, casual spot with big attractive rooms, good beach bar, south of town.

7 (tie) Tropica

Nice rooms in four-plex buildings near Banyan Bay. New pool.

7 (tie) The Tides

New, locally owned hotel with a dive orientation, at the north end of town.

9 Caribe Island Resort

Increasingly popular for those seeking a full-service small resort. South end.

10 (tie) Capricorn

Opened in 1996, this small spot on north Ambergris has three cabanas right on the beach, plus an excellent restaurant.

10 (tie) Captain Morgan's Retreat

In many ways, this is what visitors to Belize come looking for — thatched cabañas on a stretch of beach; on the north end of Ambergris Caye, next to the Essene Way. Large pool.

10 (tie) Changes in Latitudes

Canadian-run small inn near the Belize Yacht Club bills itself as a B&B. Smallish rooms, but with recent upgrades.

Other recommended spots: **El Pescador, Paradise Resort Hotel, Mata Rocks, Green Parrot, San Pedro Holiday Hotel. Exotic Caye Resort** (formerly the Playador) is under new management and is turning around.

10 Top Ambergris Condotels

For families or groups, Ambergris Caye's condotels — individually owned condos with units offered like hotel rooms by a management company —and suites hotels are hard to beat. They offer more room for not much more money than regular hotels.

1 The Palms

Well-located on the water just south of town, with attractive condo apartments, and a nice small pool.   Not to be confused with the Royal Palm, a timeshare.

2 Villas at Banyan Bay

Expanding condo development about south of town, beyond walking distance, with some of the largest and most luxe apartment units in Belize. Nice pool and beach area. Units are fully air conditioned and have jacuzzis.

3 Banana Beach

New in late 1998, this condo project by the people from Coconuts has Yucatán-style architecture and a pool. South of town beyond walking distance.

4 Mayan Princess

Convenient "mid-town" location on the water. Very good value in a suites hotel. No pool, though.

5 Belizean Reef Suites

Well-located at the south edge of town. Attractive units. No pool.

6 Belize Yacht Club
Within walking distance south of town, Mexican-style two-story units with a beautiful pool. New meeting facilities.

7 Casa Caribe
One- and two-bedroom units on North Ambergris. Nice pool and beach area.

8 (tie) Woody's/Corona del Mar
Attractive suites south of town. No pool.

8 (tie) Casa Solana
Nicely furnished, with attractive rates. No pool.

8 (tie) Emerald Reef
Very nicely designed and furnished, at north end of town. No pool.

8 (tie) Coral Bay
New suites spot south. No pool.

10 Paradise Villas
Florida-style condos at the north of town, adjacent to the Paradise Hotel, with a pool and small beach.

5 Best Budget Hotels on Ambergris

Yes, you can get a clean room on the island for under US$25 a night, even in-season. Some rooms at the following hotels cost more than that, but all offer value for the money.

1 Ruby's
The clear top choice for the budget/value traveler. Choose from new A/C units or cheaper original units.

2 Hideaway Sports Hotel
One of the few budget places in Belize with a pool. A short walk from the water. Restaurant. Variety of rooms. Some recent improvements and upgrades.

3 (tie) Lily's
Recently upgraded a bit, with A/C in some units.

3 (tie) Barrier Reef Hotel
In a colonial-era building across Front Street near Big Daddy's and Tarzan's. Pool and restaurant.

 # 3 (tie) Hotel Del Rio
Variety of rooms, under new ownership.

 # 5 (tie) San Pedrano
A favorite with European travelers, on Front Street with a breezy veranda.

 # 5 (tie) Martha's
Not on the water, but clean basic rooms at a good price.

10 Really Good Ambergris Restaurants

Ambergris Caye has some of Belize's best restaurants. We've listed our favorites in alphabetical order. Keep in mind that small restaurants can change literally overnight, with the loss of a key cook. Ask locally for the latest word.

Capricorn: Dependably delicious. Not cheap, and a bit of a trip to North Ambergris, but worth it for a special meal.
Celi's: The emphasis is on seafood. Efficient service, moderate prices.
El Patio: One of the flock of restaurants which have opened south of town. Good food and not overpriced.
Elvi's Kitchen: A little touristy, but we love it. Never had a bad meal here. The living frangipangi tree and sand floor still work for us, too.
Estelle's: Great seaside location. Breakfasts are a special treat.
Jade Garden: Perhaps Belize's best Chinese food, plus other menu choices in a pleasant setting south of town.
Mambo: Another splurge spot, at the Mata Chica resort on North Ambergris. Romantic setting, beautiful dining room. Very expensive.
The Reef: Honest Belizean food in large portions at modest prices.
Ruby's: San Pedro's version of fast food — great place for coffee and a burrito in the morning, or a home-made pie later.
Sweet Basil: Belize's only upscale deli, with scrumptious cheeses by the ounce, and good sandwiches for your North Ambergris picnic.

Special Mention: **Lion's Club Barbeque:** This is a fund-raiser for a good cause. Chicken, beans and rice, cole slaw and tortillas, every Friday and Saturday evening at the "Lion's Den" on Front Street. Several hotels also have beach barbeques -- check locally for current schedule.

Note: The status of **Rasta Pasta,** one of our favorites despite its often islow service, was uncertain as of this writing.

Honorable Mention: **Caruso, Fido's, Cannibal Cafe, Little Italy, Reality Cafe, Tropical Takeout, Popular Bakery, Ambergris Cuisine**

Mostly Mainland Travel

Photo by Marty Casado

Even mainland Belize is a land of water -- the Belize, Macal, Mopan, Sibun, New, Hondo, Sarstoon and other rivers have played key roles in the country's history

10 Top Jungle Lodges

Here are our picks for the best jungle lodges in Belize. There are so many good ones, and the difference among several of them is so small, that we're probably fools to try to rank them. You'll be happy at any of these spots. And, as well, at the ones that didn't quite make our top 10 this year.

1 Chan Chich, Gallon Jug, Orange Walk District
Barry Bowen's little lodge is smack dab in the middle of nowhere, which is exactly how guests like it. Jungle all around, birds above, Maya ruins underneath, a class operation in every direction. The Hardings do a wonderful job with management. New pool is a real plus.

2 (tie) Blancaneaux, Mountain Pine Ridge
Francis Ford Coppola's inn has a lot going for it — good food, lovely setting, luxurious villas, good management.

2 (tie) Chaa Creek, near San Ignacio, Cayo
Beautiful grounds, nearly bug-free, superbly trained staff, savvy owners, delightful for guests.

4 Ek'Tun, Cayo
Small, with only two rooms, but guests here praise this lodge to the sky.

5 Jaguar Paw, near Belmopan
Newish and luxe-ish, with 16 air-conditioned rooms; large caves and river next door.

6 Lamanai Outpost, near Lamanai ruins, Orange Walk District
The late Colin Howells built this one right and ran it like a pro. After a period of non-family management when the lodge faltered, Colin's son and daughter-in-law are back in the saddle and it's much more like it used to be. Wonderful setting on the New Lagoon.

7 Duplooy's, near San Ignacio, Cayo
This lovely small cottage colony inn is also known for its Botanical Gardens, thanks to Ken Duplooy's wonderful plantings of trees, shrubs and flowers.

8 (tie) Hidden Valley Inn, Mountain Pine Ridge
The Headley paradise on 18,000 acres offers waterfalls, streams, peace and quiet, and comfortable digs.

8 (tie) Pook's Hill, near Belmopan
Small, remote, friendly, beautiful, and a good value.

 # 10 (tie) Banana Bank, Belmopan Area
On a large working ranch; a good value and a favorite of some seasoned Belize travelers.

 # 10 (tie) Five Sisters Lodge, Mountain Pine Ridge
Beautiful setting near waterfalls and river; Belizean-owned.

 # 10 (tie) Maya Mountain, San Ignacio, Cayo
Good value, run with concern and care. New pool.

 # 10 (tie) Maruba Spa, Altun Ha Area
Not for everybody, this lodge in rural Belize District near Altun Ha appeals to Amex Platinum types with a yen for spa treatments in an exotic setting.

 # 10 (tie) Windy Hill, San Ignacio, Cayo
Near town; convenient; offers many tours; pool.

Other wonderful jungle lodges which could have made our Top 10 list, and may next time: **Warrie Head, Mountain Equestrian Trails, Nabitunich, Black Rock, Ian Anderson's** (all in Cayo), **Chau Hiix** (Orange Walk District), **Fallen Stones Butterfly Ranch** (Toledo District)

10 Top Mainland Seaside Resorts

Mainland beaches aren't Belize's strong point, but you'll have a great seaside vacation at any of these small hotels. Our top picks are very different: Inn at Robert's Grove is the new standard in upmarket accommodations in Placencia. Kitty's isn't fancy, but it has the carefree, "barefoot Belize" style that has won it legions of fans.

 # 1 Inn at Robert's Grove, Seine Bight (Placencia)
Upscale A/C rooms, beautiful pool, tennis courts, beachfront location, good new restaurant. Has expanded once already and is expanding again later in 1999.

 # 2 Kitty's Place, Placencia
Informal, barefoot spot; not fancy, but still just about perfect. Especially the beachfront cabanas. If you want to be away from things, Kitty's also has a place on French Louis Caye.

 # 3 Rum Point Inn, Placencia
A resort with character: the best guest library in Belize; unusual free-form cabins; the owners are highly knowledgeable. New units have A/C, tasteful design and are very large, though not directly on the water.

4 Luba Hati, Seine Bight (Placencia)
Beautiful grounds and outstanding design. No A/C or pool, though.

5 Jaguar Reef Lodge, Sittee Point/Hopkins
The first real resort in beautiful setting at what eventually will be another Placencia. Lots of recent upgrades, including A/C and fridges in rooms. New pool. Sandflies can occasionally be ferocious here.

6 Nautical Inn, Seine Bight (Placencia)
Rooms, in octagonal prefab units, are not at all Belizean, but the setting and service make up for it. Nice new pool.

7 (tie) Beaches and Dreams, Sittee Point
New, small spot with three cabins on the beach; early visitors say the food and ambiance are excellent here.

7 (tie) Casablanca by the Sea, Consejo (Corozal)
Watch the lights of Chetumal across the bay.

8 Serenity Resort, Placencia
Florida-style cottages and a new 10-room hotel building and a conference center; now, there's even a bar.

10 (tie) Pelican Beach Hotel, Dangriga
The Raths' hotel just to the north of town has an "Old Florida" look and atmosphere, and it makes a great jumping-off spot for the offshore cayes.

10 (tie) Sea Front Inn, Punta Gorda
Newer hotel that's making fans of guests who venture this far south.

10 (tie) Tony's, Corozal Town
An old favorite, with a great beach bar and some of the coldest air conditioning in Belize.

10 (tie) Turtle Inn, Placencia
Relax, kick-back and enjoy a little bit of the South Pacific.

Other admirable spots on the sea: **Soulshine, Singing Sands, Blue Crab, Ranguana Lodge, Green Parrot, Trade Winds** (all in Placencia)

5 Best Vacation Rentals by the Sea

Those traveling with family or in larger groups often want to rent a house. Except on Ambergris Caye, which offers both condotel and stand-alone house rentals, there are as yet few seaside vacation rentals in Belize. Here are some of the options. We have not spotlighted individual homes as there as we have not inspected most of them personally. Keep in mind that prices for rentals are often negotiable.

1 Ambergris Caye

Ambergris Caye offers a variety of one- to three-bedroom condo rentals (see our Ambergris Caye condotel list on page 81). It also has several dozen privately owned homes for rent by the week or month. Rates, especially in season, are surprisingly high, as much as US$2,000-$4,000 for properties that are attractive but not luxurious. A few homes are available for under US$1,000 a week. Probably the best source for information on Ambergris rentals is the AmbergrisCaye.com Web site. The Products and Services section of Marty Casado's site has listings, which include photos, of a number of rental properties. In addition, Caye Management is a long-established island company with rentals. Caye Villas and Los Encantos, offered by Diane Campbell, are small developments with upscale rentals available. Other real estate companies on Ambergris usually also offer some rentals.

2 Remote Cayes

Houses on Belize's remote cayes are usually modest affairs, simple cabins or cabañas, and are typically operated by a lodge on the island rather than being individually owned and rented. Among the cayes where you can find cabins, houses or cottages are Espanto, South Water, St. George's, Ranguana, French Louis, Chapel, Blackbird, Northern, Little Water, Wippari, Northeast and Tobacco cayes. To turn up specific listings, try searching the Web using the names of these cayes; also, see specific hotels and lodges in the Contacts section of this publication. The range of costs for cabins on the cayes is large, from under US$25 a day at Glover's Reef on Northeast Caye to more than US$400 a day at Cayo Espanto.

3 Placencia

As more foreigners buy real estate here, an increasing (though still small) number of homes are becoming available for seasonal or weekly rent. A good source of information is the Placencia Web site at www.placencia.com. One privately owned house about which we have received good reports is a house at the edge of Placencia Village owned by a Dutch couple, renting for US$500 a week; for information, contact Lydia's Rooms in Placencia.

4 Hopkins/Sittee Point Area

Selling lots to foreigners has been the leading industry here for several years. Only a few homes have yet been built, but already a handful of these are available for seasonal or short-term rentals. A few owners have put up Web sites about their homes, with rentals in the US$500 to $1,500 a week range.

5 Caye Caulker

Caye Caulker has an increasing number of budget apartments — starting around US$150 a week — and small cabins for vacation rentals. Heredia's Apartments and M & M Apartments are two, but you will see others as you walk around the island. Some regular hotels also offer weekly or longer rentals on their efficiency or cabin units.

10 Most Romantic Places to Stay

Any place may be romantic if you're truly in love, but here are some hotels that help the romance flow. Our selections are based on setting, general ambiance and privacy.

(Listed Alphabetically)

Blancaneaux, Mountain Pine Ridge
For those with a yen for luxury, a villa here would make a wonderful love nest — soaring thatched ceilings, indoor/outdoor Japanese-style baths, decks with views of the river.

Capricorn, North Ambergris Caye
Mini-resort with cabins on the beach and an enticing restaurant.

Casablanca, Consejo Shores
Away from the crowds, with a view of Chetumal Bay and the Mexico beyond.

Cayo Espanto, Near Ambergris Caye
Your own house with small splash pool, on a private island.

Chan Chich, Gallon Jug, Orange Walk District
For lovers with an interest in birding and wildlife.

Ek' Tun, Cayo
Two deluxe thatched cabanas for quiet times in the jungle by lamp light.

Luba Hati, Seine Bight (Placencia)
Run by an Italian, so it has to be romantic, right?

Maruba Spa, North of Belize City
A certain atmosphere of lassitude and sensuality in the jungle.

Mata Chica, North Ambergris Caye
For the hip in love.

Victoria House, Ambergris Caye
Barefoot but upmarket seaside resort — the villas here are special.

10 Places with Authentic Belizean Atmosphere

It's hard to define exactly what "Belizean" atmosphere is. What's American atmosphere? Or Canadian? Belizean can mean many different things, from the luxury of Chan Chich Lodge to a rental room in someone's home. But we'll go out on a limb here and list these places. They're all run by Belizeans and offer friendly, comfortable lodging with that little something extra called Belizean style. Most are small spots offering lodging at moderate prices.

(Listed alphabetically)
Clarissa Falls, Cayo
Belizeans flock here on weekends.

Colton House, Belize City
Alan (a British-Belizean) and wife Ondina, from Caye Caulker, run a wonderful small inn in their home across from the Radisson Fort George.

Crystal Paradise, Cayo
The Tut family have done fine things with this property.

Five Sisters Lodge, Mountain Pine Ridge
Every year, this place looks better, with lovely flowers and groundscaping.

Maya Homestay/Guesthouse Programs, Toledo
Whether you stay with a family, or in a guesthouse, it's the real Belize.

Martha's Guesthouse, San Ignacio
Well-run restaurant and budget guesthouse.

Piache Hotel, San Ignacio
Owned by a leading Garifuna family.

Pelican Beach Resort, Dangriga
Owned by members of old, prominent Belize colonial family, the Bowmans.

Tom's Hotel, Caye Caulker
Family-run budget hotel.

Trade Winds, Placencia
Run by the village's former postmistress.

5 Most Luxe Digs

Most resorts in Belize are comfortable rather than luxurious. Here are five that are both.

1 Blancaneaux (the Villas), Mountain Pine Ridge
The villa units are huge and luxurious (and pricey), with original art and appealing furnishings.

2 Cayo Espanto, near Ambergris Caye
Individual houses with splash pools.

3 Mata Chica, North Ambergris Caye
Highly designed cabañas on the beach.

4 Villas at Banyan Bay, Ambergris Caye
Condos with tasteful furnishings, whirlpools, full kitchens, and more.

5 (tie) Jaguar Paw, Belmopan Area
Rarity of rarities: air conditioning in the jungle.

5 (tie) Inn at Robert's Grove, Placencia
The new standard in luxury in Southern Belize.

Honorable Mention: **The Palms** and **Banana Beach,** Ambergris Caye; **Radisson Fort George,** Belize City

10 Great Lodging Values

These are not the least-expensive places in Belize by any means, but all offer relatively low prices and solid value for what you pay.

(Alphabetical Order)
• Clarissa Falls, Cayo
A Belizean favorite.

• Cockscomb Jaguar Sanctuary Cabins, Stann Creek
New rooms (shared bath and common kitchen) offer true jungle experience.

• Deb & Dave's Last Resort, Placencia
Clean, comfortable, friendly.

• Glover's Atoll Resort, Northeast Caye
Island camping and very basic cabins for very low prices.

• **Hok'ol K'in, Corozal Town**
While not strictly in the budget category, rooms are modern and attractive, and tour prices are among best in Belize.

• **Ocean's Edge Lodge, Tobacco Caye**
Not fancy, but a great value (with meals included) — also check out **Island Camps, Reef's End, Gaviota** and the few other spots on this 5-acre island with snorkeling right off the beach.

• **Tree Tops, Caye Caulker**
One of a number of Corker digs offering clean, safe budget sleep (also check out **Tom's Hotel, 1788 Motel, Jimiñez Cabanas, Sea View**, and others).

• **Trek Stop, Cayo**
Cozy, spic 'n span cabins just west of San Ignacio.

• **Toucan Sittee, Sittee Village**
Cabins with kitchens on the Sittee River.

• **Seaside Guest House, Belize City**
Favorite budget spot, run by the Friends, a Quaker service group.

Honorable Mention: **Wee Wee Caye; Casa Maya, Cosmos, Rose's** (all Cayo); **Conrad & Lydia's Rooms, Sea Spray** (Placencia)

5 Best Hotel Libraries

For sophisticated travelers, hotel libraries are important. Even some of the best resorts in Belize have remarkably poor libraries for their guests. One reason is that books are expensive in Belize. Here are five hotels with good libraries, most heavy on nature and ecology titles.

1 Rum Point Inn, Placencia
Superb book and video library, easily the best hotel library in Belize.

2 Hidden Valley Inn, Mountain Pine Ridge
Like the library of a country home in England.

3 Colton House, Belize City
Oriented to ecovideos and books.

4 Lamanai Outpost Lodge, Lamanai
Good selection of nature and other books.

 # 5 Chan Chich, Gallon Jug
Comfortable corner nook with books.

5 Hotels with British Honduras Atmosphere

Hurricanes, termites and time have destroyed most of the British Honduras colonial architecture. Here are some remaining jewels:

 # 1 Four Fort Street Guest House, Belize City
One of the few places in Belize City with true old-time atmosphere.

 # 2 Colton House, Belize City
A 1920 West Indies style home, one of the most charming in all of Belize.

 # 3 Great House, Belize City
Steve Maestre's renovation is a jewel.

 # 4 Manatee Lodge, Gales Point
A beautiful setting on the Southern Lagoon

 # 5 (tie) Barrier Reef Hotel, Ambergris Caye
Wouldn't it be great if all the buildings on Ambergris looked like this?

 # 5 (tie) Pelican Beach Resort, Dangriga
On the water, with verandahs.

 # 5 (tie) Cottage Colony, St. George's Caye
Collection of colonial-style cottages.

10 'Can't-Miss' Places to Eat

It's *not* true you can't get a good meal in Belize. While the country has no five-star restaurants, you can enjoy excellent seafood, and sometimes nothing tastes better than a plate of rice and beans. This list does not include resort or jungle lodge restaurants which cater primarily to guests. Some of these, such as the restaurants at Blancaneaux and Maruba Spa, are excellent. In Belize, as elsewhere, restaurants can change overnight, so always ask locally. See separate listing (page 83) for Ambergris Caye restaurants.

(Alphabetical Order)
• **Four Fort Street Guesthouse, Belize City**
The colonial ambiance is as enjoyable as the food.

• **Inn at Robert's Grove, Seine Bight (Placencia)**
Attractive new beach-front dining area at this upscale small resort.

- **La Petite Maison, Placencia**
Small and French and very, very good (closed off-season).

- **Luba Hati, Seine Bight (Placencia)**
Southern Belize's most beautiful dining room, with excellent Italian food.

- **Macy's, Belize City**
Long-time favorite for inexpensive Creole food in Belize City

- **Mango's, Belize City**
Seafood, steaks, pasta and other dishes; more upscale than most restaurants in Belize City, with a fun bar. Formerly The Grill.

- **Running W, San Ignacio**
Featuring steak and other items in the Hotel San Ignacio.

- **Sandbox, Caye Caulker**
Popular spot, with seafood and other dishes.

- **Sea Rock, Belize City**
Excellent Indian food.

- **Tony's, Corozal Town**
The upscale place to eat and greet in Northern Belize.

Honorable mention: **Cafe Kela**, Corozal Town; **Chateau Caribbean, Smokey Mermaid, Chon Saan Palace, Tela's, Marlin's,** Belize City; **Martha's Kitchen, Clarissa Falls** and **Serendib**, San Ignacio; **Kitty's Place** and **Pickled Parrot**, Placencia

5 'Must-See' Mayan Sites

Belize has literally hundreds of ruins, many still undiscovered or unexcavated. Of the dozen or so "major" ones, the wonderful thing about them is that they are almost totally untouristed. Unlike in the Mexican Yucatán or even at Tikal, where hordes of visitors swarm over the ruins, in Belize you may be alone with the caretaker, or one of only a handful of visitors, at an ancient Mayan city.

1 Caracol
The largest known site in Belize, and larger in area even than Tikal, this Classic Maya city-state was rediscovered in the 1930s but only since 1985 has excavation been underway. With an improved access road, it is now easier than ever to visit this awe-inspiring place. Caracol's highest pyramid is still the

tallest man-made structure in Belize. The drive to Caracol is beautiful and not difficult, except in wet weather. A new visitor center at the site is now open.

2 Lamanai
Lamanai was an important Maya community for three millennia, and this site has buildings dating back to 700 B.C. The setting is beautiful, at the edge of the New River Lagoon. You can drive here, via an all-weather road, though the approach by boat is inspiring.

3 Xunantunich
This Late Classic site is small but impressive. Don't miss the view into Guatemala from El Castillo, a 135-foot tower that is the second-tallest structure in Belize. A plus is its easy access from the Western Highway — you cross the Mopan River on a small hand-cranked ferry. There is a visitors center.

4 Lubaantun
Not by any means the largest, most important, or most impressive site, Lubaantun has a mysterious appeal. One reason is its setting, near the remote villages of Toledo with their population of present-day Mayans, some of whom may shyly offer to sell you crafts or small trinkets at the Lubaantun site. Another is the famous Crystal Skull, which may or may not have been discovered here in 1926 by the daughter of archeologist F. A. Mitchell-Hedges, and which may or may not be authentic. A third is the style of construction, of carefully hand-cut limestone blocks laid without mortar. Lubaantun is on an isolated ridge near the village of San Pedro Columbia off the Southern Highway.

5 Che Chem Ha Cave
Many caves in Belize contain Mayan relics. This one, on private land in Cayo District, can be visited on a guided tour. Most who make the effort to see this come away awed by the pottery which dates to the time of Christ. One access is via a long drive on the "hydro road" from Benque Viejo.

Among other highly interesting sites: **Cahal Pech, El Pilar, Altun Ha, Cerros, La Milpa, Nim Li Punit, Uxbenka**

10 Best Museums, Monuments and Natural History Attractions

Belize doesn't have much in the way of fancy museums or similar attractions, but here are 10 of interest:

1 Belize Zoo, Western Highway at Mile 29, near Belmopan
Absolutely fantastic place! One of the highlights of any kid's trip to Belize, and

fun for adults, too. See jaguars, April the mountain cow, and more, all in a natural setting.

 # 2 Government House Museum, Belize City
Grand tribute to British Honduras days of old.

 # 3 St. John's Anglican Cathedral, Belize City
Built in 1812, the oldest Anglican church in Central America.

 # 4 Natural History and Blue Morpho Butterfly Centre, Chaa Creek, Cayo
Privately operated center with growing collections of materials and displays, plus butterfly breeding center. For more butterflies, visit Green Hills, Tropical Wings and Fall Stone butterfly farms.

 # 5 Maritime Museum and Coastal Museum, Belize City
Both in the same building, the former Belize fire station. Devoted to marine and local history.

 # 6 Ambergris Museum, San Pedro
Small but fascinating.

 # 7 Tropical Wings Nature Center, San Jose Succotz, Cayo
Eco displays and a butterfly farm.

 # 8 Belize Central Bank Building, Belize City
Opened in 1998, this overblown building is a monument to government putting priorities in the wrong place.

 # 9 Cockscomb Preserve Visitor Center
Small but informative displays on Cockscomb Preserve area.

 # 10 (tie) Rainforest Trail/Ix Chel Farm, Cayo
Adjoining Chaa Creek, this private project of Rosita Arvigo highlights rain forest remedies.

 # 10 (tie) Bliss Institute, Belize City
Devoted to Belize culture, with a permanent display of Maya artifacts.

5 Dependable Car Rental Agencies

These are Belize City rental agencies which have proved to be reliable. We've had good luck with some of the other renters at the international airport, too. Regardless of which renter you choose, always check out the vehicle carefully.

Be sure the tires are good, and that there's a usable spare and a jack. Ask for the lowest-mileage vehicle available. Confirm that the company will send someone to service your car if it breaks down.

1 Budget
Good selection of late-model Suzuki vehicles; well-run and professional operation with generally dependable cars and country-wide service.

2 Crystal
A variety of cars and trucks at attractive prices, and Crystal allows its vehicles to be driven into Guatemala. Owned by a former Texan.

3 National
Suzuki and other vehicles, mostly in top shape, though prices are on the high side.

4 Jabiru
Vehicles may not be as new as at the majors, but usually they are still in good shape, with (sometimes) lower prices.

5 Hertz-Safari
Isuzu Troopers in good condition, though expensive.

Honorable Mention: **Jaguar, Thrifty, Iguana, Pancho's, Lewis, Smith's**

5 Ways to Get to Tikal

The magnificent ruins of Tikal are around 60 miles (by road) from the Belize border at Benque Viejo. This road, long paved at the Tikal end, is being further improved, with new paving from Ixlu back toward the Belize border.

1 Minivan Tour from San Ignacio
Several Belize operators offer no-hassle day and overnight tours to Tikal. Day trips, usually including guides, border fees, lunch and admission to Tikal, run about US$75 per person.

2 Fly from Belize City
Tropic Air, Maya Island Air and Aerovias fly from the international airport in Belize City to Flores (around US$160 round trip). Minibuses do the 40-mile run from Flores to Tikal. Overnight package tours, including lodging at Tikal, are available from Belize City and San Pedro, from around US$250. At some times, vans run from Belize City to Tikal (around US$25 one-way) -- ask at your hotel or check tourist bulletin boards to see if the service is available when you're there.

3 Take a Guatemala Taxi or Minibus

This is a cheaper option than a tour by a Belize operator. Walk across the border at Benque Viejo and bargain with a taxi or minivan driver in Melchor. A good price is around US$10 per person one way.

4 Take a Guatemala Bus

Buses (Pinita and Rosita lines) leave every hour or two from Melchor, starting early in the morning. Fares to either Flores or Puente Ixlú near El Remate (where you'll have to change buses to Tikal) are around US$2.

5 Drive

Most Belize car rental agencies won't let you take vehicles into Guatemala, but a couple, including Crystal in Belize City and Western in San Ignacio, do permit it.

5 Good Hotels Near Tikal

There are three hotels in Tikal National Park, close to the ruins: Jungle Lodge, Tikal Inn and Jaguar Inn. You may get more hotel for less money in El Remate, about 20 miles from Tikal.

1 Hotel Westin Camino Real Tikal, El Remate

The most upmarket hotel in the Petén, the Westin Camino Real is located in a somewhat remote area in the Biotopo Cerro Cahuí. Lakeside setting, with tennis, swimming pool and many amenities.

2 La Mansion del Pajara Serpiente, El Remate

Attractive 10-room hotel with gardens overlooking the lake and two swimming pools. Good restaurant.

3 Jungle Lodge, Tikal

In Tikal National Park, the Jungle Lodge offers two types of accommodations — 12 rooms in the budget category and 34 pleasant rooms in duplex cabañas, with a pool.

4 Tikal Inn, Tikal

Also in the park, with thatched cabañas and a pool.

5 La Casa de Don David, El Remate

Run by American-born David Kuhn, with plenty of atmosphere at low prices. Recent improvements include new rooms, electricity and restaurant. Budget rooms have shared bath.

Living in Belize

Photo by Marty Casado

The dream of living by the Caribbean Sea has wide appeal, but the reality of being an expat in a developing country is not for everyone

10 Best Places to Live in Belize

Many North Americans and Europeans have a dream of living where the water is blue, the air is warm, the rum is cheap and the living is easy. Belize may, or may not, live up to your expectations in those regards. Many who do make the leap to Belize end up frustrated, unhappy and broke, so investigate thoroughly before you decide to move to Belize. Expats in Belize are now clustered mostly in San Pedro, Placencia, the Belize City suburbs and near Corozal Town. Here are our own picks for the best places to live and buy in Belize.

1   Corozal Town/Consejo
Most visitors to Belize either never get to Corozal or pass through quickly en route somewhere else. But the Corozal Town area and nearby Consejo offer a lot for those staying awhile — low prices, friendly people, a generally low-crime environment, the beautiful blue water of the bay, and the extra plus of having Mexico next door for cheap shopping.

2   Rural Cayo District
Cayo has a lot going for it: wide open spaces, cheap land, few bugs and friendly folks. This might be the place to buy a few acres and grow oranges.

3   Hopkins/Sittee Point
This is what Placencia was 20 years ago, almost as pretty and even friendlier. If you want a place on or near the beach, prices are still relatively affordable here, but as anywhere in Belize, do your "due diligence" before putting out cash.

4   Ambergris Caye
This is the most popular, but most expensive, place for expats to live in Belize. For some, it's too touristy, but others love the fact that there are other North Americans in residence. North Ambergris will eventually be the hot spot here, though that's a bridge and several years off.

5   Toledo District
If you can stand the rain and the mosquitoes, the far south of Belize has some of the lowest land prices and nicest people in the country. When the paving of the Southern Highway is finally completed, it will open this area up to a new blush of tourism and development.

6   Placencia Peninsula
Placencia has boomed and busted before, but this time it looks like the boom will continue. Lots of lots being sold; few homes yet built.

7   Rural Orange Walk District
Orange Walk Town isn't such a wonderful place, but out in the district, around

August Pine Ridge or beside a lagoon, you may find your little piece of isolated paradise.

8 Sarteneja
If you don't mind being near the ends of the earth, the Sarteneja peninsula is a beautiful area.

9 Remote Cayes
The days of buying your own private island for a song are long gone, but if you have money to burn and the willingness to rebuild after the next hurricane, one of Belize's 200+ remote islands could be yours.

10 Caye Caulker
Corker's fans are legion, although property here is tightly controlled and rarely sold to outsiders.

5 Questions to Answer Before Moving

1 "Do I really know what it's like?"
Come down for a long visit before making a commitment; rent before you buy.

2 "Do I really know what it costs for me to live in Belize?"
Belize has not one but several costs of living, depending upon your lifestyle. Spend some time in Belize on a trial run to see what your actual living expenses will be.

3 "Am I willing to always be an outsider?"
Most expats in Belize are never fully integrated into Belize life — culturally, politically or otherwise.

4 "Do I know what precautions to take against crime?"
As a "wealthy" outsider (in the eyes of most Belizeans), you're fair game for all types of scams, ripoffs, robberies and worse. The police usually do their best, but their best may be just to take your report after the crime. You'll have to be proactive to protect yourself and your property.

5 "What will happen if I get sick?"
Belize has some excellent doctors, dentists and other health care professionals, who will treat you at lower cost than what you've probably been paying, but they're stretched thin, and supplies and modern equipment are often lacking. If you become seriously ill, what will you do? Go back home? Are you prepared to accept Belizean standards of care, go to Mexico or what?

5 Questions to Ask about Real Estate

 # 1 "What is the Belizean price?"
In Belize, there's usually a Belize price and a foreigner price. The story is often told that one's second house in Belize is twice as nice as the first and costs half as much.

 # 2 "Can I ever sell it?"
It's easy to buy in Belize but sometimes hard to sell. Remember that the local Belize market is thin, and you'll most likely have to sell to a foreign buyer. How many of them are there?

 # 3 "What will happen when the next hurricane comes?"
It's not a matter of if there will be a hurricane, but when. Is your property likely to be seriously affected?

 # 4 "What will happen to my property when I'm not in the country?"
Unless you buy a condo, you can't just lock up and leave. You'll likely come back to a house stripped of everything that can be moved. You'll need to hire a caretaker. Even with a condo, if you're not there to take care of things yourself, you're at the mercy of a management association.

 # 5 "What happens if the Belize currency is devalued?"
You're buying with hard currency, but your real estate asset is valued in Belize dollars.

5 Real Estate Firms

Keep in mind that real estate salespeople in Belize are not licensed in the same way they are "back home." Do your due diligence before investing any money in Belize real estate. Here are 5 established real estate firms:

(Listed alphabetically)
Belize Land Consultants, Consejo Shores (Corozal)
Belize Real Estate/W. Ford Young Real Estate, Belize City
Regent Realty Ltd., Belize City
Southwind Properties, San Pedro
Sunrise Realty, San Pedro

Index of Contacts

The following are mentioned in the lists. Information, where available, includes Belize or other postal address, telephone and fax numbers, e-mail and Web addresses.

AIRLINES
American Airlines, New Road at Queen St., P.O. Box 1680, Belize City; 501-2-32522; tel. in U.S. 800-433-7300; www.aa.com
Continental Airlines, 32 Albert St., Belize City; 501-2-78227, fax 2-78114; tel. in U.S., 800-525-0280; www.continental.com
Maya Island Air, P.O. Box 458, Belize City; 501-2-31140, fax 2-35371; tel. in U.S. 800-521-1247; mayair@btl.net; www.belizenet.com/mayair
TACA Airlines, 41 Albert St., Belize City, 501-2-77185, tel. in U.S., 800-535-8780; www.grupotaca.com
Tropic Air, P.O. Box 20, San Pedro, Ambergris Caye; 501-2-6-2012, fax 2-62338; tropicair@btl.net

BOAT CHARTERS
Belize Aggressor Fleet, P.O. Box 1470, Morgan City, LA 70381; tel. 800-348-2628 or 504-385-2628, fax 504-384-0817; info@aggressor.com; www.aggressor.com
Belize River Lodge, P.O. Box 80, Swan Valley, ID 83449; tel. in U.S. 888-275-4843; worldfishn@worldnet.att.net; www.belize.com/belizeriverlodge.html
Crewed Charters, 5100 Long Bay Road, St. Thomas, USVI 00802; tel. 800-522-3077 or 340-776-4811, fax 340-776-3074; crewedcharters@worldnet.att.net
Hughes, Peter Diving, 1390 South Dixie Hwy., Ste. 1109, Coral Gables, FL 33146, tel. 305-669-9391 or 800-932-6237, fax 305-669-9475; dancer@peterhughes.com; www.peterhughes.com
Offshore Express, Coral Beach Hotel, San Pedro; tel. 501-2-62817, fax 2-62864; forman@btl.net; www.ambergriscaye.com/coralbeach/index.html
Singfield, Peter Charters, Xaibe Village, Corozal District; tel. 501-4-35213; snkm@btl.net; www.www.ambergriscaye.com/reefcrawl/index.html
TMM (Belize) Ltd., Coconut Drive, San Pedro; tel. 501-2-63026, fax 501-2-63072; tmmbz@btl.net; www.sailtmm.com/Belize/beaut2.htm
Windsong Charters, Ltd., 926 West 6th Ave., Denver, CO 80204; tel. 303-983-3739, fax 303-623-7352; windsong@windsongcharters.com; www.windsongcharters.com
Winnie Estelle, San Pedro; tel. 501-2-62394; winnie_estelle@yahoo.com; www.ambergriscaye.com/winnieestelle/index.html

BUTTERFLY FARMS
Blue Morpho Butterfly Center, Chaa Creek Cottages, P.O. Box 53, San

Ignacio; tel. 501-9-22037, fax 9-22501; chaacreek@btl.net; www.belizenet.com/chaacreek.html
Fallen Stones Butterfly Ranch, P.O. Box 23, Punta Gorda; tel./fax 501-7-22167
Green Hills Butterfly Farm, Mile 8, Mountain Pine Ridge Road, Central Farm, Cayo; tel. 501-9-23310
Tropical Wings Butterfly Center, San Jose Succotz, Cayo; tel. 501-9-32265 ; susa@btl.net; tbcnet.com/dyaeger/susa/tropwing.htm

CAR RENTAL AGENCIES
Budget, 771 Bella Vista, P.O. Box 863, Belize City; tel. 501-2-32435, fax 2-30237; jmagroup@btl.net; www.budget-belize.com
Crystal, Mile 1 1/2 Northern Hwy., Belize City; tel. 501-2-31600, fax 2-31900; crystal@btl.net; www.crystalbelize.com
Hertz-Safari, P.O. Box 1737, Belize City; tel. 501-2-35395, fax 2-30268; safari@btl.net
Jabiru, 5576 Princess Margaret Dr., Belize City; tel. 501-2-44680, fax 2-34136
National, Mile 4 1/2, Western Hwy., Belize City; tel. 501-2-31650, fax 2-31586; bravo_inv@btl.net; www.belizenet.com/nationalcar.html

DIVE SHOPS
Amigos del Mar, P.O. Box 53, San Pedro; tel 501-2-62706, fax 2-62648; amigosdive@btl.net ; www.ambergriscaye.com/amigosdive/index.html
Blue Hole Dive Center, San Pedro; tel. 501-2-62982; bluehole@btl.net; www.bluedive.com
Frenchie's Diving Services, Caye Caulker; tel. 501-2-22234
Gaz Cooper's Dive Belize, P.O. Box 96, San Pedro; tel. 501-2-63202; tel in U.S. 800-499-3002, fax 954-351-9740; gaz@btl.net; www.divebelize.com/divebelize/contact.html
Hustler Tours and Pro Dive Shop, San Pedro; tel. 501-2-62279, fax 2-63468; hustler@btl.net; www.ambergriscaye.com/hustler/index.html
Patojo's Scuba Center, San Pedro; tel. 501-2-62283, fax 2-63797; patojos@btl.net; www.ambergriscaye.com/tides/index.html
Placencia Dive Shop, Placencia Village; tel. 501-6-23313, fax 6-23291; pds@btl.net; www.belizenet.com/pds.html
Rum Point Divers, Placencia; tel. 501-6-23239, fax 6-23240; rupel@btl.net; www.rumpoint.com
Sea Horse Dive Shop, Placencia Village; tel. 501-6-23166, fax 6-23166; seahorse@btl.net; www.belizescuba.com

HOTELS, BELIZE
Alajuila Suites, Barrier Reef Dr., San Pedro; tel. 501-2-62791, fax 2-62362
Anchorage Hotel, P.O. Box 25, Caye Caulker; tel./fax 501-2-22304;

tourism@cayecaulker.org.bz

Banana Bank Lodge, Mile 47 1/2 Western Hwy., P.O. Box 48, Belmopan; tel. 501-8-12020, fax 8-12026; bbl@btl.net; www.bananabank.com

Banana Beach, San Pedro; tel. 501-2-63890 fax 2-63891; bananas@btl.net; www.bananabeach.com

Barracuda & Jaguar Inn, Placencia; tel. 501-6-23330, fax 6-23250; wende@btl.net; www.belizenet.com/barracuda

Barrier Reef Hotel, P.O. Box 34, San Pedro; tel. 501-2-62075; barrierreef@btl.net; www.ambergriscaye.com/barrierreef/index.html

Beaches and Dreams, Hopkins (P.O. Box 193, Dangriga); tel./fax 501-5-37078; dreams@btl.net; www.beachesanddreams.com

Belize Odyssey, Caye Caulker, P.O. Box 460, Belize City; tel. 501-2-44277, fax 2-32580; vega@btl.net; www.belizeodyssey.com

Belizean Reef Suites, Coconut Dr., San Pedro; tel./fax 501-2-62585; bzreef@btl.net; www.ambergriscaye.com/bzreef/index.html

Belize Biltmore Plaza, Mile 3, Northern Hwy., Belize City; tel. 501-2-32302, fax 2-32301

Belize River Lodge, P.O. Box 80, Swan Valley, ID 83449; tel. in U.S. 888-275-4843; worldfishn@worldnet.att.net; www.belize.com/belizeriverlodge.html

Belize Yacht Club, P.O. Box 62, San Pedro; tel. 501-2-62777, fax 2-62768; bychotel@btl.net; www.belizeyachtclub.com

Bellevue Hotel, 5 Southern Foreshore, P.O. Box 428, Belize City; tel. 501-2-77051, fax 2-73253; fins@btl.net; www.belize.com/bellevue.html

Blancaneaux Lodge, Mountain Pine Ridge, P.O. Box B, Central Farm, Cayo; tel. 501-9-23878; fax 9-23919; blodge@btl.net; www.belizenet.com/blancaneaux.html

Blackbird Caye Resort, tel. in U.S. 888-271-3483 or 305-9697945; fax 305-969-7946; dive@blackbirdresort.com; www.blackbirdresort.com

Black Rock Lodge, P.O. Box 48, San Ignacio, Cayo; blackrock@blackrocklodge.com; www.blackrocklodge.com/blackrocklodge_com.htm

Blue Marlin Lodge, South Water Caye, P.O. Box 21, Dangriga; tel. 501-5-22243, fax 5-22296; tel. in U.S. 800-798-1558; marlin@btl.net; www.bluemarlinlodge.com

Bob's Paradise, Monkey River; tel. 501-6-12024; tel. in U.S. 954-429-8763; bobsparadise@webtv.net; www.bobsparadise.com

Bull Frog Inn, 25 Halfmoon Ave., P.O. Box 28, Belmopan; tel. 501-8-22111, fax 8-23155

Cahal Pech Village, San Ignacio, Cayo; tel. 501-9-23740; fax 9-2225; daniels@btl.net; www.belizenet.com/cahalpech.html

Captain Morgan's Retreat, San Pedro; tel. in U.S. 800-447-2931, fax 218-847-0334; information@captainmorgans.com; www.ambergriscaye.com/captmorgan/index.html

Capricorn, P.O. Box 65, San Pedro; tel. 501-2-62809, fax 2-12091;

capricorn@btl.net; www.ambergrsicvaye.com/capricorn

Caribbean Villas, San Pedro; tel. 501-26-2715, fax 011-501-26-2885; c-v-hotel@btl.net; www.ambergriscaye.com/caribbeanvillas/index.html

Caribe Island Resort, San Pedro; tel. 501-2-63233, fax 2-63399; ccaribe@btl.net; www.ambergriscaye.com/caribeisland/index.html

Casablanca by the Sea, Consejo Village, Corozal District; tel. 501-4-12018, fax 501-4-23452; info@cbbythesea.com; www.cbbythesea.com

Casa Caribe, San Pedro, U.S. office 8750 Gladiolus Dr., #166 Fort Myers, FL 33908; tel. 800-770-6844, fax 941-433-2919; casainfo@casacaribe.com; www.casacaribe.com/index.html

Casa Solana, P.O. Box 19, San Pedro; tel 501-2-62100, fax 2-62855; casasolana@btl.net; www.ambergriscaye.com/casasolana/index.html

Cayo Espanto, P. O. Box 90, San Pedro, tel./fax 501-2-13001, in U.S. 888-666-4282; info@aprivateisland.com; www.ambergriscaye.com/cayoespanto/index.html

Chaa Creek Cottages, P.O Box 53, San Ignacio, Cayo; tel. 501-9-22037; fax 2-2501; chaacreek@btl.net; www.chaacreek.com

Chan Chich Lodge, Gallon Jug, P.O. Box 37, Belize City; tel. 501-2-75634, fax 2-76961, tel. in U.S. 800-343-8009; info@chanchich.com; www.chanchich.com

Changes in Latitudes B&B, San Pedro; tel./fax 501-2-62986; latitudes@btl.net; www.ambergriscaye.com/latitudes/index.html

Chateau Caribbean, 6 Marine Parade, P.O. Box 947, Belize City; 501-2-30800, fax 2-30900; chateaucar@btl.net; www.chateaucaribbean.com

Chau Hiix Lodge, P.O. Box 1072 Sanford, FL 32772; tel. in U.S. 800-654-4424 or 407-328-7874, fax 407-322-6389; chauhiix@belize-travel.com; www.belize travel.com

Chocolate's, Caye Caulker (P.O. Box 332, Belize City); tel. 501-2-22151

Clarissa Falls, San Ignacio, Cayo; tel. 501-9-23916

Cockscomb Jaguar Preserve -- reservations through Belize Audubon Society

Coconuts, P.O. Box 94, San Pedro; tel. 501-2-63500, fax 2-63501; coconuts@btl.net; www.ambergriscaye.com/coconuts/index.html

Coral Bay Villas, P.O. Box 1, San Pedro; tel. 501-2-63003, fax 2-63006; cbayvillas@btl.net; www.ambergriscaye.com/coralbayvillas/index.html

Corona del Mar/Woody's, P.O. Box 37, San Pedro; tel. 501-2-62055, fax 2-62461; corona@btl.net; www.ambergriscaye.com/coronadelmar/index.html

Cottage Colony, St. George's Caye (PO Box 428, Belize City) tel. 501-2-12020 fax 2-73253; fins@btl.net; www.belize.com/bellevue.html

Crystal Paradise, Cristo Rey, Cayo; tel./fax 501-9-22772

Deb & Dave's Last Resort, Placencia Village; tel. 501-6-23207, fax 6-23334; debanddave@btl.net

Dem Dat's Doin', Punta Gorda; tel. 501-7-22470

duPlooy's, San Ignacio, Cayo; tel. 501-9-23101; fax 9-23301; duplooys@btl.net; www.duplooys.com

D-Victoria Hotel, 40 Belize Corozal Rd., P.O. Box 74, Orange Walk Town; tel. 501-3-22518; 3-22847; dvictoria@btl.net ; www.d-victoriahotel.com

Ek 'Tun Lodge, Macal River, Cayo; tel. 501-9-2002, tel. in U.S. 303-442-6150; info@ektunbelize.com; www.ektunbelize.com

El Pescador, P.O. Box 17, San Pedro; tel. 501-2-62398, fax 2-62977 pescador@btl.net; www.elpescador.com/index.html

Embassy Hotel, Belize International Airport, P.O. Box 1931, Belize City; tel. 501-2-2226, fax 2-52267; bzemhtl@btl.net

Emerald Reef Suites, Sandpiper St., San Pedro; tel. 501-2-62306; fax 2-62806; travltour@btl.net; www.belizenet.com/emerald.html

Exotic Caye Resort/Playador, San Pedro; tel 501-2-62870, fax 2-62871; tel. in U.S. 800-201-9389; playador@btl.net; www.ambergriscaye.com/playador/index.html

Fiesta Inn, Kings Park, Belize City; tel. 501-2-32670, fax 2-32660; fiestainbz@btl.net; www.fiestainnbelize.com

Five Sisters Lodge, Mountain Pine Ridge, 29 Theodocio Ochoa St., San Ignacio, Cayo; tel. 501-9-23184; fivesislo@btl.net

Four Fort Street Guest House, P.O. Box 3, Belize City; tel. 501-2-30116, fax 2-78808; fortst@btl.net; www.fortst.com

French Louis Caye — contact via Kitty's, Placencia

Gaviota Coral Reef Resort, Tobacco Caye; tel. 501-5-22085

Glover's Atoll Resort, Northeast Caye; tel 501-1-48351 or 5-12016; glovers@btl.net; www.belizemall.com

Great House, 13 Cork Street, P.O. Box 85, Belize City; tel. 501-2-33400, fax 2-33444; greathouse@btl.net; www.greathousebelize.com

Green Heaven Lodge, P.O. Box 155, San Ignacio; tel./fax 501-9-23641; ghlodge@ghlodgebelize.com; www.ghlodgebelize.com

Green Parrot Beach Cottages, 1 Maya Beach, Placencia; tel./fax 501-6-22488; greenparot@btl.net; www.belizenet.com/greenparrot

Green Parrot, P.O. Box 36, San Pedro; tel./fax 501-2-12096; gparrot@btl.net; www.ambergriscaye.com/greenparrot/index.html

Hidden Valley Inn, Mountain Pine Ridge, P.O. Box 170, Belmopan; tel. 501-8-23320, fax 8-23334; tel. in U.S. 800-334-7942; info@hiddenvalleyinn.com; www.hiddenvalleyinn.com

Hideaway Sports Lodge, P.O Box 43, San Pedro; tel. 501-2-62141, fax 2-6-2269; e-mail hideaway@btl.net; www.ambergriscaye.com/hideaway/index.html

Hok'ol K'in Guest House, P.O. Box 145, Corozal Town; tel. 501-4-23329, fax 4-23569; maya@btl.net

Holiday Hotel, Barrier Reef Dr., P.O. Box 61, San Pedro; tel. 501-2-62014, fax 2-62295; holiday@btl.net; www.ambergriscaye.com/holidayhotel/index.html

Hopkins Inn, Hopkins; tel. 501-5-37013; hopkinsinn@btl.net

Hotel Del Rio, San Pedro; tel./fax 501-2-62286; hodelrio@btl.net;

www.ambergriscaye.com/hoteldelrio/index.html
Iguana Reef Inn, P.O. Box 31, Caye Caulker; tel. 501-2-22213, fax 2-22000;
iguanareef@btl.net; www.iguanareefinn.com
Inn at Robert's Grove, Seine Bight, Placencia; tel. 501-6-23565, fax 6-
23567, info@robertsgrove.com; www.robertsgrove.com
Jaguar Paw Lodge, Belmopan; tel. 501-8-13023, fax 8-13024; tel. in U.S.
888-775-8645; cyoung@jaguarpaw.com; www.jaguarpaw.com
Jaguar Reef Lodge, Hopkins; tel./fax 501-2-12041; jaguarreef@btl.net;
www.jaguarreef.com
Journey's End, 4 1/2 Mile North Ambergris, P.O. Box 13, San Pedro; tel.
501-2-62173, fax 2-62397; info@journeysend.com;
www.ambergriscaye.com/journeysend/index.html
Jungle Drift Lodge, Bermudian Landing; tel. 501-1-49578
Kitty's, Placencia (P.O. Box 528, Belize City); tel. 501-6-23227, fax 6-23226;
info@kittysplace.com; www.belizenet.com/kittys
Lamanai Outpost Lodge, P.O. Box 63, Orange Walk; tel./fax 501-2-33578;
lamanai@btl.net; www.lamanai.com
Lillpat Sittee River Lodge, Hopkins (P.O. Box 136, Dangriga); tel. 501-5-
12019, fax 5-12019; lillpat@btl.net; www.lillpat.com
Lily's, San Pedro; tel. 501-2-62059; lilies@btl.net;
www.ambergriscaye.com/lilys/index.html
Lighthouse Reef Resort, P.O. Box 1435, Dundee, FL 33838; tel. 941-439-
6600 or 800-423-3114, fax 941-439-2118; reservations@scubabelize.com;
www.scubabelize.com
Little Water Caye Resort, Little Water Cayc; tel. 501-6-12019, fax 6-12019;
littlewate@btl.net; www.bclizecaye.com
Luba Hati, Placencia (P.O. Box 1997, Belize City); tel. 501-6-23402, fax 6-
23403; lubahati@btl.net; http://www.lubahati.com
Manatee Lodge, Gales Point -- contact through Hidden Valley Inn
Manta Resort, tel. in U.S. 800-326-1724; info@mantaresort.com;
mantaresort.com
Martha's Hotel, P.O. Box 27, San Pedro; tel. 501-2-62053, fax 2-62589
Martha's Guesthouse, 10 West St., P.O. Box 140, San Ignacio, Cayo; tel.
501-9-23647; marthas@belizex.com
Maruba Spa, Maskall Village, Mile 40, Old Northern Hwy.; tel. 501-23-
22199; www.4windstravel.com/shows/belize/maruba.html
Mata Chica, San Pedro; tel. 501-2-13010, fax 2-13012; matachica@btl.net;
www.ambergriscaye.com/matachica/index.html
Mata Rocks, P.O. Box 47, San Pedro; tel. 501-2-62336, fax 2-62349;
matarocks@btl.net; www.ambergriscaye.com/matarocks/index.html
Maya Guest House and EcoTrail Program, Punta Gorda; tel. 501-7-22119
Maya Mountain Lodge, San Ignacio, Cayo; tel. 501-9-22164, fax 9-22029;
nature@mayamountain.com; www.mayamountain.com
Miller's Landing, Placencia; tel. 501-6-23010, fax 6-23011;

mlanding@btl.net
Mopan River Resort, Riverside North, Benque Viejo del Carmen, Cayo; tel. 501-9-32047, fax 9-33272; mopanriver@btl.net; www.mopanriverresort.com
Mountain Equestrian Trails, Pine Ridge Rd., Cayo; tel. 501-9-23310, fax 8-23361; AW2trav2Bz@aol.com; www.belizenet.com/MET/methp.html
Mayan Princess, San Pedro; tel./fax 501-2-62778; mayanprin@btl.net
Nature's Way Guesthouse, 65 Front St., Punta Gorda; tel. 501-7-22119
Nautical Inn, Seine Bight Village, Placencia Peninsula; tel. 501-6-23595, fax 6-23594; nautical@btl.net; www.nauticalinnbelize.com
Ocean's Edge Lodge, Tobacco Caye; tel. 501-1-49633
Palms, The, Coconut Dr., San Pedro; tel. 501-2-63322, fax 2-63601; palms@btl.net; www.ambergriscaye.com/palms/index.html
Paradise Villas, P.O. Box 49, San Pedro; tel. 501-2-63077, fax 2-62831; cayeman@btl.net; www.ambergriscaye.com/paradisevillas/index.html; also offering units here is **Tradewinds Paradise Villas,** San Pedro; tel. 501-26-2822, fax 2-63746, tel. in U.S. 800-451-7776; bze@msn.com; www.ambergriscaye.com/paradise/index.html
Paradise Resort Hotel, San Pedro; tel. 501-2-62083, fax 2-62232; paradise@btl.net; www.ambergriscaye.com/paradiseresort/index.html
Pelican Beach Resort, P.O. Box 2, Dangriga; tel. 501-5-22044, fax 5-22570; pelicanbeach@alt.net; www.pelicanbeachbelize.com
Piache Hotel, 18 Buena Vista St., San Ignacio; tel. 501-9-22032
Pine Ridge Lodge, P.O. Box 2079, Belize City; tel 501-9-23310
Placencia Lagoon Resort, Malacate Beach, Independence, Stann Creek; tel. 501-6-22363, fax 6-22482
Pook's Hill, P.O. Box 14, Belmopan; tel. 501-8-12017, fax 8-23361; pookshill@btl.net; www.belizenet.com/pookshill.html
Radisson Fort George, 2 Marine Parade, P.O. Box 321, Belize City; tel. 501-2-33333, fax 2-73820, tel. in U.S. 800-333-3333; rdfgh@btl.net; www.radissonbelize.com
Ramon's Village, Coconut Dr., P.O. Box 51, San Pedro; tel. 501-2-62071, fax 2-62214, tel. in U.S. 800-624-4215; info@ramons.com; www.ambergriscaye.com/ramons/index.html
Reef End Lodge, Tobacco Caye; tel. 501-5-22419
Rose's Guest House, Cahal Pech Hill, San Ignacio; tel. 501-9-22282
Royal Palm, P.O. Box 18, San Pedro; tel. 501-2-62148, fax 2-62329; royalpalm@btl.net; www.belize.com/royalpm.html
Ruby's, P.O. Box 56, San Pedro; tel. 501-2-62063, fax 2-62434; Rubys@btl.net; www.ambergriscaye.com/rubys/index.html
Rum Point Inn, Placencia; tel. 501-6-23239, fax 6-23240; tel. in U.S. 800-747-1381; rupel@btl.net; www.rumpoint.com
San Ignacio Resort Hotel, P.O. Box 33, San Ignacio, Cayo; tel. 501-9-22034, fax 9-22134; sanighot@btl.net; www.sanignaciobelize.com
San Pedrano, Barrier Reef Dr., San Pedro; tel. 501-2-62054, fax 2-62093

Sea Beezzz, Caye Caulker; tel. 501-2-22176
Sea Front Inn, P.O. Box 20, Punta Gorda; tel. 501-7-22300, fax 7-22682;
seafront@btl.net; www.belizenet.com/villoria/seafront.html
Seaside Guest House, 3 Prince St., Belize City; tel. 501-2-78339
Seaview Hotel, P.O. Box 11, Caye Caulker; tel. 501-2-22205;
106303.245@compuserve.com; www.belizenet.com/seaview
Serenity Resort, Placencia; tel. 501-6-23232, fax 6-23231; serenity@btl.net;
www.serenityresort.com
Seven Seas Hotel, San Pedro (1443 Del Prado Blvd., Cape Coral, FL 33990);
tel. 800-458-8281 or 941-574-7755, fax 941-574-5500;
traveler@tourandtravel.com; www.sevenseas-belize.com
1788 Motel, P.O. Box 17, Caye Caulker; tel. 501-2-22388, fax 2-22153
Shirley's Guest House, P.O. Box 13, Caye Caulker; tel. 501-2-22145, fax 2-
22264; shirley@btl.net; www.belizenet.com/shirley.html
Spanish Bay Resort, Spanish Lookout Caye; tel. 501-2-77288;
sbrturton@btl.net
Soulshine, Placencia; tel. 501-6-23347, fax 501-6-23369;
caribe@soulshine.com; www.soulshine.com
St. George's Lodge, St. George's Caye. (P.O. Box 625, Belize City), tel. 501-2-
12121; sgl.belize@btl.net; www.gooddiving.com
SunBreeze, Coconut Dr., P.O. Box 14, San Pedro; tel. 501-2-62191, fax 2-
62346; e-mail sunbreeze@btl.net;
www.ambergriscaye.com/sunbreeze/index.html
Sunset Beach Resort, San Pedro; P.O. Box 416, Decatur, TX 76234; tel. 501-
2-2373, fax 2-62562; tel. in U.S. 940-627-2514; jowinmew@wf.net;
www.ambergriscaye.com/sunsetbeach/index.html
Tate's Guesthouse, 34 José Maria Nuñez St., Punta Gorda, tel. 501-722568
Tides Beach Resort, San Pedro; tel. 501-2-62283, fax 2-63797;
patojos@btl.net; www.ambergriscaye.com/tides/index.html
Toledo Host Family Network, Punta Gorda; tel. 501-7-22470
Tom's Hotel, Caye Caulker; tel. 501-2-22145
Tony's Inn & Beach Resort, P.O. Box 12, Corozal Town; tel. 501-4-22055,
fax 4-22829; tonys@btl.net; www.belizenet.com/tonysinn/
Toucan Sittee Lodge, Sittee River, Stann Creek; tel. 501-5-22888
Trade Winds Hotel, Placencia Village; tel. 501-6-23122
Tree Tops Hotel, P.O. Box 29, Caye Caulker; tel. 501-2-22008, fax 2-22115;
treetops@btl.net
Tropica, San Pedro; tel. 501-2-62701, fax 2-62699, tel. in U.S. 973-835-2350;
vacation@tropicabelize.com; www.tropicabelize.com
Turneffe Flats Lodge, Blackbird Caye; tel. in U.S. 800-815-1304;
tflats@btl.net
Turneffe Island Lodge, Caye Bokel (P.O. Box 2974, 454 Greene Street,
Gainesville GA 30501); tel. in U.S. 770-536-3922 or 800-874-0118, fax 770-
536-8665; info@turneffelodge.com; www.turneffelodge.com

Turtle Inn, Placencia; tel. 501-6-23244, fax 6-23245; turtleinn@btl.net; www.turtleinn.com

Victoria House, P.O. Box 22, San Pedro; tel. 501-2-62067, fax 2-62429; tel in U.S. 800-247-5159; info@victoria-house.com ; victoria@btl.net; www.victoria-house.com

Villas at Banyan Bay, P.O. Box 91, San Pedro; tel. 501-2-63739, fax 2-62766; banyanbay@btl.net; www.banyanbay.com/html/villas.html

Warrie Head Ranch and Lodge, P.O. Box 244, Belize City; 501-2-70755, fax 2-75213; bzadventur@btl.net; www.warriehead.com

White Ridge Inn, Gales Point (P.O. Box 62, Dangriga); tel. 501-1-47150; bramey@btl.net; www.belizenet.com/whiteridge

Windy Hill Resort, San Ignacio, Cayo; tel: 501-9-22017, fax 9-23080; windyhill@btl.net; www.windyhillresort.com

HOTELS, GUATEMALA

Jungle Lodge, Parque Nacional Tikal; tel 502-926-0519, fax 476-8775

La Casa de Don David, El Remate; tel. 502-926-0269 (community telephone)

La Mansión del Serpiente, El Remate; tel. /fax 502-926-0269 (community telephone)

Jaguar Inn, Parque Nacional Tikal; tel. /fax 502-926-0065

Westin Camino Real Tikal, El Remate; tel.502-331-2020, fax 337-4313; tel. in U.S. 800-278-3000,

MEDIA

Amandala Newspaper, 3304 Partridge St., Belize City; tel. 501-2-24703; russell@btl.net; belizemall.com:80/amandala/

Channel 5/Great Belize Productions, P.O. Box 679, Belize City; tel. 501-2-73146, fax 2-74936; gbtv@btl.net ; www.channel5belize.com

LOVE-FM Radio, 33 Freetown Rd., Belize City; tel. 501-2-32098; lovefm@btl.net

The Reporter Newspaper, P.O. Box 707, Belize City; tel. 501-2-72503, fax 2-78278; report@btl.net; www.bze.net/reporter/

San Pedro Sun Newspaper, P.O. Box 35, San Pedro; tel. 501-2-62070; sanpdrosun@btl.net; www.ambergriscaye.com/sanpedrosun

ORGANIZATIONS/STORES

Belize Audubon Society, P.O. Box 1001, Belize City; tel 501-2-35004, fax 2-34985; base@btl.net; www.belizeaudubon.org

Belize Bank, Market Square, Belize City; tel. 501-2-77132. fax 2-72712

Belize Tourism Board, New Central Bank Building, Level 2, Gabourel Lane, P.O. Box 325, Belize City; 501-2-31913 or 800-624-0686; fax 2-31943; info@travelbelize.org; www.travelbelize.org

Belize Tourism Industry Association, 10 N. Park St., P.O. Box 62, Belize City; tel. 501-2-72464, fax 2-78710

Belize Zoo, P.O. Box 1787, Belize City; tel./fax 501-8-13004; belizezoo@btl.net; www.belizezoo.com
Bowen & Bowen, Ltd., 1 King St., Belize City; tel. 501-2-77031, fax 2-77062
Brodie, James & Co. Ltd., Albert & Regent Sts., Belize City; tel. 501-2-77070, fax 2-75593; brodies@btl.net
Embassy of Belize in the United States, 2535 Massachusetts Ave., NW, Washington, DC 20008, tel. 202-332-9636, fax 332-6888
Embassy of the United States in Belize, 29 Gabourel Lane, P.O. Box 286, Belize City; tel. 501-2-77161, fax 2-30802; embbelize@state.gov; www.usemb-belize.gov
Monkey Bay Wildlife Sanctuary, P.O. Box 187, Belmopan, tel. 501-8-23180, fax 8-23235; mbay@pobox.com
Save U Supermarket, San Cas Plaza, Belize City; tel. 501-2-31291, fax 2-33927

REAL ESTATE
Belize Land Consultants, P.O. Box 35, Corozal Town, tel. 501-4-12005, fax 4-12006; www.consejoshores.com
Belize Real Estate/W. Ford Young Real Estate, P.O. Box 354, Belize City; tel. 501-2-72065, fax 2-31023
Caye Management, P.O. Box 49, San Pedro; tel. 501-2-63088; cayeman@btl.net
Regent Realty Ltd., 81 North Front St., Belize City; tel. 501-2-70090, 2-72022; regent@btl.net; www.regentrealtybelize.com
Southwind Properties, San Pedro; tel. 501-2-62005, fax 2-62331; southwind@btl.net; www.ambergriscaye.com/southwind/index.html
Sunrise Realty, P.O. Box 80, San Pedro; tel. 501-2-63737, fax 2-63379; sunrise@btl.net; ambergriscaye.com/sunrise/index.html

TOUR OPERATORS
International Expeditions, One Environs Park, Helena, AL 35080; tel. 800-633-4734 or 205-428-1700, fax 205-428-1714; belize@ietravel.com; www.ietravel.com.
International Zoological Expeditions, 210 Washington St., Sherborn, MA 01770; tel. 800-543-5343 or 503-655-1461, fax 503-655-4445; ize2belize@aol.com,; www.1ze2belize.com.
Island Expeditions, 368-916 W. Broadway, Vancouver, BC, V5Z 1K7 Canada; tel. 800-667-1630 or 604-452-3212; info@islandexpeditions.com; www.islandexpeditions.com
Magnum Belize, P.O. Box 1560, Detroit Lakes, MN 56502; tel. 800-447-2931 or 218-847-3012, fax 218-847-0334,; information@magnumbelize.com; www.magnumbelize.com.
Slickrock Adventures, P.O. Box 1400, Moab, UT 84532; tel. 800-390-5715, fax 435-259-6996; slickrock@slickrock.com; www.slickrock.com